MW00744744

Bringing up a

Dream Child

Discipline Your Child
Without Shouting Or Spanking

Juhi Aggarwal

UNICORN BOOKS

Publishers
UNICORN BOOKS, New Delhi-110002

E-mail: unicornbooks@vsnl.com
Website: www.unicornbooks.in • www.kidscorner.in

Distributors
Pustak Mahal, Delhi
J-3/16, Daryaganj, New Delhi-110002
☎ 23276539, 23272783, 23272784 • *Fax:* 011-23260518
E-mail: info@pustakmahal.com • *Website:* www.pustakmahal.com

London Office
5, Roddell Court, Bath Road, Slough SL3 OQJ, England
E-mail: pustakmahaluk@pustakmahal.com

Sales Centre
10-B, Netaji Subhash Marg, Daryaganj, New Delhi-110002
☎ 23268292, 23268293, 23279900 • *Fax:* 011-23280567
E-mail: rapidexdelhi@indiatimes.com

Branch Offices
Bangalore: ☎ 22234025
E-mail: pmblr@sancharnet.in • pustak@sancharnet.in
Mumbai: ☎ 22010941
E-mail: rapidex@bom5.vsnl.net.in
Patna: ☎ 3294193 • *Telefax:* 0612-2302719
E-mail: rapidexptn@rediffmail.com
Hyderabad: *Telefax:* 040-24737290
E-mail: pustakmahalhyd@yahoo.co.in

© **Copyright : Unicorn Books**

ISBN 81-780-6035-3

Edition : 2007

Printed at : Unique Colour Carton, Mayapuri, Delhi-110064

Preface

Is parenting

- a pleasure or a pain?
- an art or science?
- invigorating or monotonous?
- creative or passive activity?

There is no joy comparable to parenthood! There is no greater joy than having loving, independent, free-thinking, well-adjusted, self-motivated, and self-disciplined children.

Children often exhibit inappropriate behaviour like screaming, shouting, whining, throwing temper tantrums, answering back insolently at public places and at home. Parents end up looking embarrassed, frustrated and helpless. Most often, the root cause of this kind of behaviour is ineffective discipline. A different kind of disciplinary approach has to be used in different situations. This book tells you how, when, where and who should discipline the child. Implement the techniques and be prepared to be complimented on the excellent upbringing of your children.

How to Use This Book

This book provides more than twenty-two hints on how you can create a conducive atmosphere at home to establish a feeling of mutual trust with the child. It tells us how we, the parents who are the role models for the children, exhibit inappropriate behaviour in front of them. It tells us fifteen ways in which we can avoid a verbal war or conflict. It tells us ways in which we can reason with the child. It shows how we can tell the child the outcome of his behaviour and pave the way for self-improvement. It also deals with ways in which we can lift our sagging spirits in this twenty-four-hour physically and mentally taxing job.

Try to read one or two tips everyday, implement them and watch out for results.

Happy Parenting!

Acknowledgement

I wish to dedicate this book to my parents, hoping they feel that their daughter has fulfilled their dreams.

I wish to thank my two sisters, Neena and Neeru, who are also my best friends, confidants and well wishers.

My two lovely children Ashna and Ayush are the inspiration behind this book.

My husband Atul is my pillar of strength.

Last but not the least, I would like to thank Dr. Ashok Gupta for his constant encouragement and invaluable guidance.

—Juhi Aggarwal

Contents

Introduction

"A fifteen-year-old commits suicide, fearing poor performance in boards, unable to meet the high expectations of his parents."

"An eleventh class student creates a pornographic website featuring his classmates and teachers."

"An eleven-year-old girl mothers a child," scream the headlines of newspapers. At parent-teacher meetings, you may come to know about the rebellious behaviour of students, like bunking classes, stealing, lying, smoking, behaving insolently or bullying. Your friend pours out the troubles she has with her children. "She takes pleasure in doing just the opposite of what I say. She has turned into a total rebel. My son is a television addict and does not listen to me at all." Such a sorry state of affairs is quite disheartening.

Parents want the best in life for their children. They put in their best. A major part of their time and effort is directed towards their child. They may be greatly involved, but if the interaction with their child is not properly managed, its very purpose could be defeated. Parents may feel embarrassed, frustrated or defeated. The root cause of all these problems could be ineffective discipline and lack of communication.

Children come first and foremost in our list of priorities. Taking good care of them and raising them in a healthy environment is our most important responsibility. Bringing them up is a unique, creative activity that involves intensive, personalised and long-lasting care. Parenting implies integrating the head, heart and hand of the child. It is not inherent; it's an art that has to be cultivated.

Sometimes, with the mounting pressure of everyday life, even simple situations seem very difficult. At these times we wonder why we are deliberately (and happily) working as slaves; spending anxious hours, sleepless nights, exhausting days, and coping with mentally taxing schedules. A gentle hug and a handmade card, with 'World's best father or mother' written on it, could be the answer to all your questions.

Sometimes, when as adults we are dealing with our children, we tend to forget our own childhood, its joys and sorrows, its pleasures and difficulties. Splashing in a muddy puddle, burrowing in sand, frolicking in the rain, and finger painting, etc. give immense joy to children but might seem useless to parents.

Discipline

Discipline does not mean undue restriction.

My mother-in-law's favourite line is, "These two of yours seem to require more attention than six of mine ever did." Coping with two, present-day kids is not easy, for they are more aware, active and demanding. Right kind of discipline is one of the keys to a happy home and is essential for the proper development and well-being of every child.

Most of us are very fortunate. We usually do not experience any major trouble with our children. But if we look closely at parents with troubled children, ineffective discipline seems to be the underlying cause for all the problems.

The following facts should be helpful while dealing with children, but it should be remembered that discipline neither begins nor ends with yelling, shouting, hitting, slapping or punishing.

1. Good Discipline is not Punishment

Punishment can make the child feel angry, rebellious or confused. It might not even curb the undesirable attitude in the child.

2. Good Discipline Involves Giving Specific Instructions

Giving specific and clear-cut instructions will assure good behaviour and curb inappropriate conduct. Clarity in instructions will certainly regulate their behaviour.

3. Discipline is not Perfect

Every child is unique in his own way. He is not a puppet. You cannot pull strings all the time to manipulate his behaviour. The child is growing. He is acquiring new skills every day. Parenting is a tough job. Parents should not hope to have total control over the child. It is best to have a healthy parent-child relationship so that the child can be taught what he needs to know.

4. Discipline is an Ongoing Process

Disciplining does not begin at any specific time, say meal time or homework time. It is an ongoing process. Do not give instructions all the time, a frown or a raised eyebrow can do the job.

5. Discipline does not Mean Stifling the Child

Too many dos and don'ts stifle the natural behaviour of the child. When children are allowed to learn from their mistakes, they tend to mature in a better manner and are able to face life in a better way.

6. Discipline Varies with Age, Needs and Situation

How well your disciplining techniques work depends a lot on the child's age, special needs or prevailing circumstances. Sometimes an idea works, sometimes it may not.

Try different ways. Take tips from relatives and close friends and keep trying till the problematic behaviour lessens and is ultimately given up. Your bag of tricks should be like 'Dadi Ma Ki Pitari', which had a simple household cure for every ailment.

There are numerous simple and non-violent ways of disciplining a child. But many parents hit their children; in fact, most do. We can very well assume by this that they have tried their best but have been unable to cultivate good manners and proper behaviour in the child. The parents do not realise that hitting has more negative effects than positive ones. They can try various methods listed here.

What is Hitting?

It is the infliction of pain on the child's body because he has made a mistake or has acted in a disobedient manner. In a fit of rage, the person might pick up a stick, scale, belt, slipper, brush or whatever he can lay his hands on, which he might regret later. An older person normally punishes a younger one. The child may respond by crying, screaming or by just staring back insolently.

Why should Hitting be Avoided?

1. Hitting is not Effective

Throughout our lives we wish children, people and events to be just the way we want them to be. When they are not, we get angry. We create tensions and physical punishment becomes a way to let off steam and serves as an outlet of our own deep seated anger rather than a controlling measure. For a short while, on being hit, the child might do what we want him to, but in the long run, it will become ineffective.

I know of a doctor couple who wanted their only son to take up Medicine, so that he could take over their successful practice later on. The son was more inclined towards computers. When discussions, persuasion and rewards failed, they resorted to physical punishment to change his mind. The son got such a setback that he fared poorly in the secondary exams and was ineligible to take up Medicine.

When a parent physically punishes a child, he may feel guilty and sorry later. On the other hand, children might get the message that problems can be solved by violence. Later in life, whenever they are faced with a problem they cannot cope up with, they may use the same violent way to deal with it, instead of adopting a pragmatic and mature manner.

2. Hitting can be Dangerous

Hitting can cause severe *physical or psychological damage*. A child may suffer temporary pain or may even be wounded. Remember, wounds tend to leave scars. Hitting a child on the face or head can cause permanent damage to eyes, ears, teeth or even brain.

Children who are hit repeatedly may become obstinate, unyielding, sullen, uncompromising and resolute. They might display signs of extreme anger or aggressive behaviour. They may suffer from recurrent nightmares. They may no longer respond to verbal appeals. They may even feel that they are bad – not that their behaviour is bad – and may suffer from low self-esteem, and develop an inferiority complex.

There is an old saying that when your shoe starts fitting in your son's feet, it's time to treat him as a friend. Teenagers may turn hostile when beaten. Under extreme provocation they might also just hit back. I have even seen a two-year-old hitting back at parents in public. The look of embarrassment on the parents' face was quite evident. The reasons for such behaviour need analysis.

3. Hitting Leads to More Violence

Here I cite the example of an elite well-to-do family, living in a posh area. The fourteen-year-old was getting into regular fights with the neighbours and domestic help. He picked up quarrels with the guards, gardeners, servants, neighbourhood children, and even passers-by. He had an edge over the working force not because of his greater physical strength, but because of his family's status. He got away with a lot of hitting and kicking. The parents were surprised to hear about the complaints.

On a closer look it came to light that the father sometimes resorted to wife-beating or child-beating in a fit of drunken rage. The wife was not averse to hitting the maid. The fourteen-year-old had umpteen violent fistfights with his older brother. The parents used corporal punishment to discipline the child. Physical violence was just a part of daily life in the family.

This child learnt from his family that hitting could solve many problems. To deal with stressful situations, one could use one's fists. He learnt that one could hammer one's point across by using force. The person who had more physical strength could subdue or dominate the other person. So, in turn, he used similar tactics with his neighbours and the people around him.

4. Hitting is Unlawful

Although the Indian law (Penal code) does not have any specific laws against child abuse, it is a crime to harm the child in any way. Physical abuse may be described as any act by an adult that results in non-accidental physical injury to the child. Uncontrollable fury can sometimes result in injury. In other countries, children are even taken away from their parents by the state in extreme cases.

Disciplining is a serious matter. You have to take important decisions on how you will discipline your child. This book offers you a host of new ideas, options and tactics so that you can make the best possible decisions. If you follow simple basic advice offered in this book, parenting will become a pleasure and not a pain in the neck.

Child Abuse

Some stressful situations like unemployment, poor housing, job dissatisfaction, marital disputes, disobedient children and so on, can contribute to deep parental frustration and tension and probably to child abuse. Some parents might use excessive physical force in an attempt to discipline children by beating, hitting, pushing, throwing them down, or even suffocating them. Parental brutality does not serve any purpose. It is an expression of their own feelings of frustration and unhappiness; a reaction to the intolerable conditions of their own.

Unfortunately, child abuse is widespread and appears to be on the increase. It has been observed that *parents who abuse their children were themselves abused or neglected as children.*

A child who is a victim of abuse is likely to become a highly aggressive adult later in life. Erratic or inconsistent discipline may serve to escalate aggressive interchange, which is bound to become more intense and abusive with time.

Parental and Home Influences on Child Behaviour

Parental behaviour has a profound effect on children's psychological growth and behaviour. Social values and control are ingrained during early child-parent interaction. The foundations of a child's social attitudes and interpersonal skills are also laid at home. 'Home' is the child's first school. It is the greatest socialising agency.

Socialising the child is the process by which we want him to acquire those beliefs, behaviour, standards and motives that are valued by our society. 'Home experiences' have an important role in determining whether the child will be independent, autonomous, assertive, achievement oriented, competitive, generous, loving, socially responsive or on the other hand, dependent, self-effacing, aggressive, submissive or perverse.

Our childhood memories may be happy and cheerful, or sad and regretful. Nobody can be said to have had a perfect childhood. Nor is it possible for us to give a perfect childhood to our children. All parents have different styles of bringing up their children. Parenting styles can be broadly categorised into three types:

1. Authoritarian
2. Indulgent or permissive
3. Warm democratic

1. Authoritarian Parents

These types of parents take all decisions regarding their children. They are aggressive, dominant and strict. They seem to be very powerful and are feared constantly. They impose rigid standards of behaviour although they wish the best for their children. They are not ready to accept any changes in customs and traditions. No matter what, these parents want total obedience from their children. They believe that what they think is always correct. They try to fit them into the typical mould of a perfect child. Children of such parents might become withdrawn, cold and stubborn.

2. Indulgent or Permissive

This is a house with lenient and loving parents, but with no set rules. The child may be granted whatever he wants, irrespective of the sacrifices parents have made in fulfilling those wishes, which later become demands. The house is usually not very well maintained or organised. Punishments and rewards are erratic. Parents are lax in discipline. Sometimes the child is kept in extreme conditions of protectiveness. The child does not learn the skills required to be independent. The parental behaviour may be erratic and they may not face responsibility. Children from such homes may be self-centred, dominating and careless.

3. Warm Democratic

The parents in these families are well adjusted, vital, outgoing and enjoy children. The child is a full member of the family group and is neither pampered nor ignored.

Parents are loving and affectionate towards children. The rules in the house are neither too strict nor too lax. There is a reasonable degree of permissiveness. There is an explanation for family rules. Children are duly given satisfactory answers to their curious questions. There is avoidance of arbitrary decisions. They are taken after consultations with the family members. If the child breaks any rules, he is taken to task. The parents listen to the grievances of the child and encourage him, when he acts in an independent, mature and responsible manner. Children from such homes are extremely sociable and friendly. They are popular, secure, and adjust easily.

4. Mother's Role in Child Rearing

A mother spends more time with the child as compared to the father. Hence, she has a greater opportunity to influence the child's behaviour. Child rearing is generally recognised as a mother's privilege and responsibility. A father may see his children briefly before bedtime, on Sundays or annual vacations. However, career women tend to be over-protective, tense and demanding with regards to bringing up children.

5. Father's Role in Child Rearing

The father influences his children's behaviour in a variety of direct and indirect ways. He determines, to a large extent, the personal and social values on which family life is based. He influences the mother's attitude towards home and child management.

Nowadays, however, there is a decrease in the autocratic method of control. Parent-child rapport is encouraged. It either decreases or increases during disciplinary actions. Now, the responsibility of the father as a parent is much emphasised and treated almost at par with that of the mother.

A harmonious home, in which consistent and democratic childcare procedures predominate, should be the goal towards which all parents should strive. This would lead to their own happiness and that of their children. Well-adjusted parents have high probability of rearing well-adjusted children. They should feel good about themselves and what they do.

Siblings: They exert significant influence on a child's personality and social behaviour. He learns loyalty, sharing, helpfulness, domination and competition from his brothers and sisters.

What are Rules?

If a three-year-old is asked what is meant by a rule, he may probably reply that a rule is not to hit anybody, break anything or run around the furniture. He would define a rule as a guideline forbidding specific behaviour. For an older child, a rule is something you apply to make the place better. Rules are more like general, neutral guidelines. A small child may follow rules just to avoid negative consequences, while an older child might take it to be a social conformity. A teenager may regard it as beneficial or utilitarian. A rule may be defined as a principle to which an action must confirm. Rules provide the framework within which a child works and plays, to enable him to reach his goal safely. The aim of good parenting is to raise humane, freethinking, independent and responsible young people.

Setting Rules According to Age

Before setting any rules for children it is better to understand the child's psychology at that particular age. Children's general behavioural patterns at different stages of their development are discussed here.

Infants: Birth-2 years

Infants display a wide variety of behaviour patterns – they eat, cry, move, babble, sleep, play, smile and so on. They discover new things through their sensory organs, like eyes, ears, mouth, nose and skin. They taste, touch, smell, perceive and hear. As they grow older, their sleeping time lessens. A newborn may sleep for twenty hours while a one-year-old requires twelve hours of sleep. Their means of communication with the outer world is through crying, cooing, babbling, gurgling and smiling. Some infants are prone to crying, whining or fretting at the least provocation and are difficult to placate while others may be more tolerant. This can be probably because they come across new or strange situations which they are unable to understand or react to.

They slowly gain familiarity with people, objects and events. They may be messy, cranky or noisy. While establishing rules for them, the following points should be kept in mind:

1. Begin after fifteen months.
2. Infants learn slowly.
3. It is better to teach one rule at a time.
4. They need a lot of care and love.
5. They need consistency and familiarity.

Pre-school Children: 2-5 years

Play is an important activity at this stage. Pre-school children like to explore and experiment. They seem to have unlimited energy and curiosity. Independent behaviour of the child should be encouraged at this stage. Overall supervision, however, is a must. The places in the house where they play should be clean and safe. There should not be any sharp objects or easily breakable articles there. At the beginning of this stage, children are self-centred and can play alone with toys for hours. As they start going to play school, they learn how to get along with others. Sometimes they have difficulty in distinguishing between facts and fantasy. They may have imaginary friends or pets. Playing gives them food for thought and helps in cognitive development. Play-acting and pretence-play is very common. Enacting as 'Papa and Mummy', 'Doctor and Patient' or 'Teacher and Student' is quite common. These games can be an expression of their feelings and fears. As their imagination becomes more vivid, the games become more elaborate. Some children show a certain amount of aggression. They may hit, push or kick others. They can be very possessive and might even throw tantrums. At this stage, parents should try to resolve problems in a non-aggressive way.

School-going Children: 6-12 years

Children in this age group are more practical and flexible. They begin to understand the difference between imagination and reality. They develop new skills. They become less self-centred and can monitor their thoughts to find a solution. They can serialise, classify and relate to situations and objects. They understand relationships and are more responsible and less dependent. They need to gain confidence at this stage. They are also likely to harm or injure others or destroy objects and can act mean, in a number of ways. They need support and encouragement. Parents must be patient and liberal while dealing with them. They must encourage their child to do his best, rather than to be the best.

School-going children should be set simple goals, so that when they attain them they feel a sense of achievement, which will help to build their confidence and self-esteem. Extracurricular activities should be encouraged and a strong sense of values should be inculcated in them.

Adolescents: 13-18 years

Adolescence has long been considered a more difficult period in the growth of a child, than the middle childhood years. This is a period of rapid physical, sexual, psychological, mental and social changes, to which the young boy or girl must adjust. Teenagers have often been compared to a ship that has left the safe shores of childhood and is going to sail through rough waters of life, to reach adulthood. They may experience unkind weather, calm sea or boulders on their way. But they have to steer clear of all possible hurdles and become responsible adults. They have to determine their goals in life and learn how to achieve them. A responsible parent has to play the role of a friend, philosopher and guide. Parents have to be understanding, loving and comforting. It is in these years that a teenager is most susceptible to the vices of smoking, drugs, alcohol and sexual excesses. They have to be warned against them. Parental ties may weaken, as peers play a vital role at this stage. Parents should share their feelings and problems and must keep an eye on the kind of company their teenaged son or daughter keeps.

It should always be kept in mind that everything, including rules, is relative. They should be changed or altered as per the needs and demands of time. Keep the following things in mind, while chalking out regulations for your children:

1. Rules have to be set according to age: An eight-year-old might have to report at home at seven in the evening after play, while a teenager's deadline may be nine in the night. Matchsticks may be forbidden for a two-year-old, but for a young girl, learning cooking, handling them would be a must. A teenager's need for privacy should be respected, whereas a pre-school child would need constant supervision.

2. Rules should be flexible: This does not mean that a child can take them for granted. However, new rules and limitations may have to be set, as the child becomes older and more independent. A five-year-old may be allowed to cycle only in the driveway or the park, while a twelve-year-old can be trusted to drive along the footpath.

3. Rules have to be based on needs and level of responsibility: If a teenager is attending special coaching classes in the evening, his curfew hour may have to be extended. If the child has some special hobbies like aero-modelling or gliding, he may have to be given extra pocket money. Rules should not be too strict. Parents should move with the times. They should realise that the fads and fashions of the younger generation can be different. Understanding parents will not have to face rebellious teenagers or truant school children.

Techniques and Ways to Discipline Children

Conducive Atmosphere At Home

1. Basic Needs of the Child should be Met

The environment factors at home should be such that they promote proper physical and mental growth of the child. He should be provided with adequate food, clothing and other basic needs. There should also be an opportunity for rest and relaxation. The child should be protected from debilitating disease and physical injuries.

Food and temper are said to have a direct correlation. It is believed that soldiers in Alexander's mighty army were never fed enough. This kept them in a perpetual state of aggressive, fierce and combative mood. A simple reason behind a child's bad disposition may be the inability to voice his needs. Sometimes, hungry children get so moody that they start rejecting their food if their meals are delayed. So, make sure that they are getting three square meals a day, including other tit-bits (beware of over-indulging and over-feeding children).

A newborn may sleep eighteen hours in a day. The time required for sleep gradually decreases. By the time a child is one-year-old, he may require just ten hours of sleep but, of course, the pattern differs from one child to another. If the child does not get the required hours of sleep and rest, he can get quite irritable and cranky. Children require a minimum eight hours of sleep. Although teenagers will hate to admit it, they also require sufficient hours of rest and relaxation. A heavy schedule of schoolwork, home assignments, extra-curricular activities, sports and so on might leave them exhausted by the end of the day. Lack of sleep reduces concentration, which can affect the quality of their work. It may also make them prone to shouting, screaming, yelling and answering back. So, watch out for signs of physical fatigue in your children. A sleepy pre-school kid appearing for a kindergarten interview (necessary evil in India), on a summer afternoon, may just clam up or create such a din that the whole school management is put to a frenzy.

Temporary poor health may also be a reason for the obstinate behaviour of the child. A child who is ill is not expected to conform to every regulation. Do make necessary allowances. But make sure that he does not take undue advantage of his illness. Having a cold and cough should not increase his TV viewing time!

2. Child's Home should be a Happy Place

The child's home should be a happy place. There should be a balanced and affectionate relationship between parents and children. Children should feel secure and well adjusted in their houses. Ideally a sense of harmony should prevail at home. It should be the place where you can be yourself.

Studies show that children from happy homes are more social, outgoing and well adjusted. Children from broken homes have a sense of insecurity. They are easily distracted and are impulsive, and have a short attention span. They usually have witnessed distress and conflict early in life. Single parents are more stressed out as they have to manage both at office and at home. Single mothers may find it difficult to discipline their children, who generally regard their father as the symbol of power and authority.

Fill your house with love. The more love you give, the more you will receive. Rather than waiting for the other person to bestow love, we must be the source of love. "If you love someone, show it", a poster of a happy boy, surrounded by four affectionate puppies clambering all over him, says it all.

3. Children Need Space

Children need space to play, work, create and enjoy. If a child gets an individual room, he is lucky. Sometimes children share a room. This is a place where the child feels free. He can decorate it as he wishes and do what he likes. Space may be made available to him in the garage or garden shed, if none is available in the house. Here he can be 'himself'. He can create and explore. He can pursue hobbies, like painting, pottery, or playing a musical instrument. In small houses, children can be provided with a desk and a shelf in the living room.

In cramped quarters it is natural for people to live in tight corners and get on each other's nerves. It is difficult for a child to study in a room with his parents watching TV, and a younger sister playing with toys. Several studies have shown that children, who study in narrow, constricted places, are more likely to be quarrelsome and aggressive.

If you don't have much space, try to create it. City authorities have many well-maintained parks, and there must be one somewhere around your house. Infants in their buggies, little kids on their tricycles, boys and girls playing and enjoying themselves make a very pretty sight. Infants are known to act cranky if they are not taken for their regular outdoor strolls. And who knows, you might enjoy your walk more than the children.

4. Children Need Time for Free Play

The mercury is soaring to 45°C, it's summer break in schools. But parents have prepared an elaborate timetable for the kids. Morning 9 am to 12 am – hobby classes; afternoon 3pm to 5pm – sports coaching; evening 6 'o clock – one hour computer class, followed by swimming. Obviously, time has also to be found out for doing home assignments and other school projects. Where is the time for free play for the child?

Like *"Dadi Ma Ki Pitari"*, which had a simple household cure for every problem, parents are quite often very happy to enroll their child in a summer camp. They feel that the child would learn new skills and would be occupied in constructive activities. What they may fail to realise is that the life of the child becomes overly programmed. He has to hop from one activity to another. He may not even have time to enjoy the activities he is involved in. To top it all, he would be commuting in sweltering summer heat.

Ideally, the child should be given some time for free play. He may be far happier playing with pebbles, sticks, paper planes and so on. Children develop imagination with free play. A simple wooden stick may serve as a horse, a bat, a spoon, a paddle and what not. Therefore, parents should avoid too many dos and don'ts.

5. Parents are Role Models

Children observe and imitate their parents. They pick up words, actions and manners from them. Thus, if you want your child to read books – read them yourself; if you want him to be honest – be honest yourself; if you want him to apologise when he makes a mistake, first do so yourself. You are his *role model*, who is exhibiting various kinds of behaviour patterns. The child will learn to do the same by what he observes in you.

A person who smokes may find his two-year-old copying the same action, blowing air through his lips, with a chalk or pencil held between fingers. A woman who uses foul language while speaking to servants may find her daughter speaking in the same way, while scolding her dolls. If the parents quarrel in front of children, they may watch the same scene being enacted when the children play 'Ghar-Ghar'. No wonder, children are called little monkeys who love to ape others.

Many behavioural reactions, idiosyncrasies, attitudes and standards may be acquired without direct training or reward, through the process of identification. One common instance of this is the child acquiring the attributes of a person he admires.

There are two pre-conditions for the establishment of strong identification with the parents. First is, naturally, that of the genetically inherited physical traits, like the colour of eyes, hair texture or a particular way of walking or talking. Second, and more important, are the psychological attributes. The parents should possess some ideal qualities, which would be 'inherited' through direct observation. The children will identify readily with a warm, loving, competent or a strong parent. Though this process is unconscious, the behaviour acquired through this is more concrete and enduring. The children will identify more with the parent of the same sex, because they look and dress alike.

So, if you have a habit of reaching late for schedules, don't be surprised if your daughter becomes a latecomer at school. The irresponsible and careless attitude has simply passed on to her.

Following are some of the appropriate behaviour patterns to be modelled before children:

Infants

1. Showing love for others.
2. Understanding the meaning of the word 'no'.
3. Finishing the food in your plate.

Pre-school Children

1. Paying respect to elders by touching their feet or greeting them.
2. Keeping things at their proper place.
3. Speaking in an appropriate manner.

School-going Children

1. Being punctual and respecting deadlines.
2. Answering the doorbell and phone properly.
3. Settling disputes without quarrelling.

Teenagers

1. Understanding the importance of money and time and utilising them wisely.
2. Saying no to drugs, alcohol, sex and smoking.
3. A polite and decent way of talking.

6. Proper Selection of Play Things

"My son has a big collection of guns. Revolver, rifle, machine gun, you name it, he has it. Whenever he goes to the market, he insists on buying a new one. Last week I bought him boxing gloves, a punching bag and a new detective set," my friend was declaring rather proudly. The child's interests and choices do matter, but it is up to the parents to diversify them. Toy weapons tend to increase the aggressive tendencies of children. Studies have shown that boys who are more aggressive between 6 and 10 years of age, are more likely to become aggressive adults.

In this age of video games, computers and electronic toys, I wonder what happened to good old board games like monopoly, scrabble, chess, Chinese checkers, building blocks, modelling kits, puzzles and so on. They require active participation of the child and increase his creative skills manifold.

Sometimes children just need a gentle push or a reminder to go in the right direction. I would like to cite my own example here.

One Sunday afternoon, I sat down to play scrabble with my husband. The children were busy with their never-ending Sunday cartoons. After hearing excited voices, my son came to see what was it that we were doing. As I struggled to find a word starting with 'Z', my son quietly suggested 'Zest'. "Not fair," cried my husband, which was heard by my daughter. She joined her father, and soon all four of us were deep in this delightful game. The dictionary was consulted extensively to resolve disputes. Now my children would rather play a challenging game. of scrabble than watch cartoons endlessly.

Such games teach children how to concentrate, plan, take quick decisions and develop a competitive spirit. Here I would like to suggest some suitable games for different age groups.

0-2 years   -   rattles, soft toys, mobiles, soft ball, musical toys.

2-5 years   -   puzzles, building blocks, doll-houses, dolls, kitchen sets, cars or train sets, bat-ball, plasticine, crayons.

6-12 years   -   board games, badminton, tennis, chess, mechano, carpentry set, gardening kit, embroidery sets, carrom, painting colours and musical instruments.

31

| 13-18 years | - | sports equipment, advanced modelling kits, musical instruments, and 'hobby' kits like chemistry set or electrical gadgets set, puzzle books. |

7. Be Impartial to All

Try to be absolutely fair and impartial to all the children at home, irrespective of their age and sex. Most of us may like to state emphatically, that in our household we treat girls and boys equally, but in the corner of the mind sometimes, we do have a different set of rules for both of them. In most of the Indian homes, boys are encouraged to be assertive, independent and even arrogant, while girls are expected to be cooperative, subdued and submissive.

Fighting, hitting, teasing, bullying, giving blow for blow, are regarded as part of growing up for boys, while girls are discouraged when they exhibit such behaviour. Girls might tolerate this discrimination till a certain age, but some time they will definitely question you and argue.

"Why do I have to be home at 7 p.m. while *bhaiya* can stay out till ten?" Your daughter may question, "Why do I get less pocket money as compared to *bhaiya*?" The questions can be very piercing, especially if the children are more or less of the same age. If the parents feel that their action is justified, they should explain the reason for doing so. A proper explanation would certainly simplify matters and avoid confrontation.

So, try and be impartial and unbiased.

8. Exposure to a Wider Environment

Joint or extended family set-up provides an excellent environment for bringing up children. Grandparents, uncles and aunts often help the parents in raising them. They can provide emotional support in the hour of need.

The child interacts with so many people of different age groups. Children love to listen to stories from their grandparents. They get abundant learning opportunities to learn new things from elders. Interacting with half a dozen cousins enhances their social skills.

You can enroll him in group activities like scouting, trekking, theatre and so on. Interacting with children of his own age group, where all of them work, play, eat, read and sleep together will enhance his independence and induce within him a sense of responsibility.

Introduce him to the world of books. He would never feel lonely or bored again. Books are a person's best friend, who will never abandon him. Let him read fiction or non-fiction. Reading a newspaper is a must for any person. A child can be taught to read headlines from age six onwards. From then on, he would start his own learning process.

9. Providing a Variety of Stimuli

Sometimes children get extremely bored with a single activity, say building blocks or painting or anything else. In frustration, they may vent their anger on blocks or paints, scattering or throwing them. They can vent their anger on other children or even adults. Symptoms of self-aggression, like pulling one's own hair or banging fists on the wall are not uncommon among pre-school kids. The general attention span of a school-going child is less than 30 minutes. If forced to continue with the same activity, he may lose all interest in it.

Frequent change in the activity is a must to refresh or invigorate the child. Reading, followed by listening to music or going for a walk is a good idea. If the same activity has to be followed for a longer period, it is best to have small breaks in between. Let's suppose that he has to do thirty mathematics problems in a day. He can take a break after ten problems, and get himself a glass of lemonade; after twenty problems, he may talk to his friend over the phone and so on. The task would be complete in no time.

10. Select Suitable Goals

Select such goals for children that may satisfy their needs and are within their reach. In majority of the cases, a child is able to accept the limitations of his abilities after reasonable effort. It is advisable to hang the basketball net a little lower in the beginning, and increase its height, as the child grows taller.

I have seen enthusiastic, first-time parents trying to teach a two-year-old to write. A child of this age is not physically mature even to hold the pencil properly. He is most likely to hold the pencil in his palm. To be able to recite a poem or two at this stage is a reasonable expectation.

The long-term goal may be split up into several short-term goals, so that the child experiences a sense of achievement when he reaches one. If a ten-year-old has to memorise a long poem, it is better to split it up into five parts of two stanzas each. Each day the child can memorise one part and by the end of the week, he would have learnt the whole poem.

Similarly, making a child learn all the colours at once is impossible. It is advisable to start with one colour every week. Let's say, 'red'. During this whole week, red-coloured objects should be pointed out to him, so that the concept of red gets firmly implanted in his mind. The next week, another colour, 'yellow', can be taken up, and so on.

The long-term goals should be chosen according to the child's talent, interest, potential and capability. After all, not all forty students in a class can become computer engineers or doctors. Assess your child's strengths. As he grows older, he may want to choose his own goals, which may be different from those selected by you. Accept his goals and help in the achievement of those goals.

A reasonable level of failure in pursuit of the goal should be tolerated. What you should note, however, is the amount of sincere effort that was put into it.

Personal satisfaction in one's chosen direction is more important than attaining goals set by the parents.

Remember, if the individual goals are not attained, it will lead to frustration, and this frustration may be directed towards oneself or others. It is at this time, that the parents need to lend their support to their child. They can listen to his feelings and console him. Failure makes one mentally and emotionally weak. Parents should stand besides their child at such moments, and encourage him to try again and not lose heart.

11. Have a Proper System in the House

Everyone appreciates a neat and clean house. Everything should be placed at the suitable place in the house. The system of placement should be simple, reachable and logical. It will be easier for you to run a systematic home and also easier and safer for the child. If things are not kept in their proper place, they are likely to get lost or spoilt and can even cause accidents.

In many households, just ten minutes after their arrival from school, children turn the house upside down. Shoes and water bottle are thrown at one corner and school bag at the other; school uniform is scattered all over the room and lunch is accompanied by TV. How much easier would life be, if children were taught to place things in their proper place: uniform in the laundry bag for washing, shoes in the shoes rack, bag on the desk and so on.

Dusting, sweeping and mopping should be done daily. It is also necessary to stop clutter from accumulating. We Indians, I think, are the biggest accumulators of clutter. A cluttered house reduces efficiency, besides giving an untidy look.

Every family member has to show active involvement in keeping the house clean and systematic. These habits should be inculcated in the child from an early age. They cannot be taught overnight. It is not a one-time job, but an ongoing process. Good habits should be encouraged and bad habits should be frowned upon.

How you can arrange for the child's articles to be placed systematically, is explained as follows:

Infants
A plastic or reed tub, bucket or basket to keep all those rattles, teethers, balls and toys.

Pre-school Children
Shelves or racks to place puzzles, board games, kitchen sets, story books, paints and so on. The shelves should be at a low, reachable level and should not be crowded.

School-going Children
They can have separate desks in well-lit places with drawers, and text books, reference books or painting equipment may be put in them. In addition to the desk, they need storage space to keep their sports equipment.

Teenagers

In addition to a bigger desk (which may be required for placing the computer), space for keeping musical instruments, books and so on.

All the storage spaces should be such that they are readily accessible. The child should have no difficulty in the removal or placement of things.

The clothes cupboard, with school uniform on one side and other clothes on the other, is easy to manage. The drawers can house the socks and handkerchiefs. Undergarments and nightwear can be kept in a separate pile. The bathroom can have a laundry bag or a bucket for keeping soiled clothes.

You may have to lend a hand, once or twice a month, to rearrange things and keep them in order.

12. Play with Your Child

How many of us have ever actually played with our children? Throwing the dice absentmindedly or tossing the ball with office work on the mind do not count. Do play with your child. Time spent with children is never wasted. Play with your child before he gets too old to play with you. Enjoy the time spent with your child. You may not get another chance.

Clear your mind and put your problems at bay. Focus exclusively on the child and show him that you care. Children need your attention, and sometimes they will misbehave, just to attract it. This phenomenon is usually witnessed when younger siblings are born. Older children feel jealous due to lack of attention. By spending time with your child, you are telling him that you love him and he is important to you. Playing encourages healthy mental and physical attitude. This can help you to identify his talents and sharpen his skills.

Try some of the following games with your children and see how they make a difference.

Infants
1. Peek-a-boo.
2. Making objects appear and disappear.
3. Clapping, making different noises.

Pre-school Children
1. Simple board games like ludo.
2. Playing with a ball.
3. Play-acting.

School-going Children
1. Baking a cake.
2. Planting saplings.
3. Playing pictionary.
4. Playing chess.

Adolescents
1. Jogging together.
2. Unscrambling the crossword.
3. Dancing or singing.
4. Going together for mountain trekking, camping, other expeditions.

Spending time with your child is an excellent way of relaxing yourself, and at the same time getting to know him really well.

13. Find Something to Praise

Praise is a very effective medium. It can work wonders. A child who feels good about himself has better chances of success than one who does not. Nurturing self-esteem is the central element in inspiring a child to perform well. But self-esteem is not built in a day; it has to be worked upon, bit by bit, day by day.

Remember, praise does not mean flattery. Also, a child is quick to detect false praise. Finding something to praise at a time when everything seems to go wrong, is indeed difficult. Praise boosts the morale of the child. It encourages him to try again, even if he has failed. It shows him that his parents believe in him. It encourages him to achieve better results.

My son was very excited when he was chosen for his class cricket team. However, to his disappointment, he did not bat a single ball or bowl a single over. "I am going to leave the school team," he announced with finality and out of desperation. "Well, I heard from your friend, Pulkit, that you took a brilliant catch at mid-on. You are surely going the Jonty Rhodes way," I remarked. "With more practice, I am sure they will promote you in the batting line-up." Encouraged and pleased with himself, my son now looked forward to his next batting practice sessions.

14. Catch Them Young

"Time to put your toys away, toys away, toys away," sang my sister. To my surprise her one-and-half-year-old daughter gathered all her scattered toys in the room and put them in the toy basket. "Time now to wash our hands, wash our hands, wash our hands and off we go to the park," sang my sister. The child washed her hands in the little sink gleefully. "One-and-a-half years may seem too tender an age to train a child, but believe me, children do understand simple commands," said my sister. "Initially I spent ten minutes everyday in trying to teach her how to pick up her toys, while I could have done the same in two minutes but, then, how am I to expect that she would do her chores and not expect me to do them, when she grows up?"

Children of this age can be taught to say 'Sorry', 'Thank you', 'Please', 'May I', at appropriate occasions. These are habit-forming concepts. Be sure to use these words frequently in front of them. The next time you say "thank you" to your kid, he may just reply with "mention not".

15. Establish an Atmosphere of Trust

The atmosphere at home should be comforting. The child should feel that his parents are always there for him. He should feel their support and security and feel free to come to them with his little problems, which may seem to have huge proportions for him.

My friend's thirteen-year-old daughter seemed subdued and miserable for the last two-three days. In the evening when mother and daughter were alone, the mother talked to her comfortingly. She burst out crying. "Mummy, the other day when I was coming home from my tuition class, a boy squeezed my breasts and ran away. It happened so fast that I couldn't do anything. Nothing worse is going to happen to me or is it?" Her mother held her tight and talked to her about the ways of the world. She told her how she could detect the ill intentions of people and ward off any unbecoming advances.

My fifteen-year-old nephew had been coming late once a week, on the pretext of extra classes in school. My sister pampered him with hot drinks and nutritious snacks as soon as he came home. On one such day, he hugged my sister and said, "Mom, I am sorry. I was going to the movies with my friends. I wasn't having any extra classes. You have complete faith in me. I can't deceive you. In the future, I will tell you honestly where I am going."

16. Give Them Relevant Information

I was sitting in a bus behind two eleven-year-old girls and I couldn't help overhearing their conversation. One girl was saying to the other, "I am feeling very scared. I think I have got some rare type of cancer. Don't tell anyone, I have been noticing blood spots in my underwear since the last two days. I am having terrible abdominal pain. I haven't told anyone about this. I don't know what to do." The child had been torturing herself with unnecessary fears. Her mother should have told her about the menstrual cycle and how it is a part of growing up and a completely normal phenomenon.

Even today, parents in India are reluctant to talk with their children about the natural physical developments of the body. When a girl turns ten or eleven, it is the right time to tell her about the changes that will occur in her body. You can take the help of a good book, which has illustrations. Explain in detail to her about the menstrual cycle, growth of reproductive organs, growth of breasts, pubic hair, etc. Similarly, a boy of thirteen or fourteen years should be provided information about growth of reproductive organs, facial hair, voice change and so on. Fathers should lay to rest fears pertaining to uncontrolled erection or initial ejaculation.

It is better that children get accurate and complete information from reliable sources, like teachers and parents, rather than obtaining inaccurate information from unreliable sources like friends, magazines and internet.

When a teenager is forewarned about the changes which are going to take place in his or her body, the child accepts them readily and these changes may even become a source of pride rather than anxiety or confusion.

17. Children Need Privacy

It is imperative that parents keep an eye on the activities of their children, but at the same time they should not breathe down their necks, specially with teenagers. Set time limits for them. Twenty-four-hour supervision is not necessary. In fact, they feel irritated if put under this kind of surveillance.

My fifteen-year-old niece has a separate bedroom for herself. She says her mother becomes frantic even if she locks it for an hour. "Honestly aunt, I don't know what Mummy thinks I am doing. You know I am very much interested in dress designing. I just wear different dresses, do up my hair differently and walk around. Mother does not understand my behaviour. Am I not old enough to do what I want in my room for an hour?"

Privacy is an important aspect of sexual development. Fascination with the body is normal in teenagers. They are very conscious about their appearances. You should never tease or ridicule a child about the physical changes taking place in him or her.

Do not ask a teenager to give a minute-by-minute account of his or her activities. Trust them, but be alert for any unexpected changes in their behaviour.

18. Give Concrete Evidence

Teenagers have to be made aware of the dangers of smoking, alcoholism and drugs. They also have to be warned of the dangers of being promiscuous. Random and indiscriminate sexual relationships can result in casualties, which affect the mind as well as the body. Teenagers have to be given information about AIDS and other sexually transmitted diseases.

Teenagers do have information about these subjects, but it is usually half-cooked facts, which may be incorrect, incomplete and confusing. Parents can help them in a number of ways: marking out articles in newspapers and health magazines, which deal with these topics, underlining important lines, for instance, "Every cigarette you smoke shortens your life by five minutes", "Choose health not disease, avoid drinking", "Stop smoking, lungs at work", and so on. On World AIDS day or anti-smoking day and the like, make the children participate in debates, discussions, seminars, and poster-making competitions on the ill effects of smoking, drugs and alcoholism. Children absorb information in a better way, if shared amongst peers.

Select programmes from TV and radio, in which experts talk about these subjects. Even if he is able to register a single message, through a half-an-hour programme, consider yourself successful in your attempt.

Give examples from life. If any of your friends, acquaintances, neighbours or relatives has suffered ill health due to any of these problems, do tell about it to your teenager. State it simply. "Do you know that Uncle Sharma's liver has suffered 50 per cent damage? He used to have two drinks a day. Now the doctor has forbidden him from drinking completely." Or, "Have you noticed

Mr. Arora's incessant cough? He has been a chain smoker for the last five years", and so on.

Surveys and studies conducted on teenage sexual behaviour provide concrete evidences to show that teenage pregnancies are detrimental for both the mother and the child and how unprotected sex can invite a host of problems.

Last but not the least, Hindu scriptures have divided the human life into four 'Varnas' (stages). The very first stage among them is 'Brahmacharya', followed from birth to twenty-five years of age. This is the time for learning, making a place for yourself in the society and earning. Any other activity distracts you from your goal. Try to explain this to a teenager in simple terms. Worldly pleasures should take a back seat, till the first stage is over.

19. Turn Negative Beliefs into Positive Beliefs

A child is always idealistic. He expects everything to be beautiful and perfect. As he grows, he finds ugliness, injustice and imperfection. These may leave him frustrated, doubtful and disillusioned. A teenager may feel angry or cynical.

He may feel, "I am ugly" or "Everybody cheats in exams" or "Hard work never pays", "Maths is beyond me" or even "Why work hard, World War III is round the corner, let me enjoy the time which is left". These kinds of negative beliefs have to be changed to positive ones.

Talk to him, be open to questions, explore feelings, do not ridicule, and ask him to list his positive traits. Ask him to work out a solution, which he thinks would work. Discuss things with him. You can instill positive beliefs in him, by telling him, "You look very pretty when you smile" or "Those who cheat never prosper, they may temporarily succeed" or "Hard work always pays off", "You can improve your maths if you get some help and work regularly at it", "World War III may take time, meanwhile prepare for your board exams".

20. Step in Their Shoes

You may feel that life is easier for your child than it was for you, what with all the modern gadgets and facilities. Just compare a day in your childhood to that of your child. Your routine was school and then free play. Their schedule is school-homework-tuition-T.V.-study-study and more study. Look at the tremendous pressures on them. Unending syllabus, fierce competition, meeting assignment deadlines and at the same time, excelling in extracurricular activities.

With the number of children in families being restricted to two or even one, all parental aspirations start resting on a single child. I have seen children becoming nervous wrecks when their examination answer sheets are being distributed, after being evaluated. Teachers are pressurised and cajoled to increase marks. Battles are fought even for half a mark. You see, children are answerable to their parents. Parents compare their marks with those of their peers. If they are even a little lower than them, it results in scolding, shouting and punishment. A sensitive child may be traumatised. This will increase his performance related anxiety next time, which, in turn, can lead to poorer marks.

Before tackling a problem, it is a good idea to assess the feelings of the child. Is he tired, upset, disturbed or unfocused? A different approach has to be followed in each case.

21. Choosing Peer Groups Carefully

As the child enters teenage, his bond with the parents becomes weak and he seeks greater independence. He may find it difficult to share his problems with his parents. He may feel that his parents are 'old-fashioned', or that there is a 'generation gap' between them.

His friends talk the same language. They enjoy and share similar fashion, fads and music. He wants the support and acceptance of his peers. If the teenager is neglected at home, he is pushed even further towards his peer group.

A great deal of caution has to be exercised while assessing his friends. One way is to invite them over for small get-togethers. Observe them, converse with them and find their views about different things. Talking in general with the child, when he comes back from school or college, will also give you a lot of information about his friends. If you find that your ward's friends are engaged in smoking, drugs, cheating, eve teasing or any such activity, it is time to act.

The first step can be a gentle warning on these lines, "You are known by the company you keep. If anything goes wrong, the whole group will be blamed. You cannot plead innocence then or put blame on others. The whole group will have to share the punishment."

The second step can be pointing out the disadvantages of bad company. Point out examples of some teenagers who have failed to achieve success due to bad company. All this has to be done very carefully and tactfully.

A friend of mine warned her fifteen-year-old son about an undesirable friend. He stopped speaking to his mother for a few days and instead stuck to his friend. The mother was extremely worried. She just didn't know what to do.

She told her son that he could meet his friend, provided he came to their house. This did not suit his friend. He did not like adult scrutiny on his unsavoury activities. Slowly their friendship dwindled. The son realised that his mother wanted the best for him and his friend was misleading him.

22. Look Out for Major Personality Changes

The rush of hormones in adolescence causes teenagers to have mood swings and experience restlessness. All this is perfectly normal.

However, keep an eye on changes in sleep patterns, decreased appetite, withdrawal from friends, angry outbursts, fearfulness, self-destructive behaviour and overwhelming guilt. The child may show feelings of utter hopelessness, despair and have a preoccupation with the concept of death. Psychologists point out that these major personality changes may be the initial signs of suicidal tendencies.

Immediate action must be taken in such cases. It is best to involve child-counsellors. A third party intervention may prevent a mishap. Immature minds sometimes make mountains out of molehills. All their doubts and unnecessary fears should be laid to rest. They have to be told that life does not end with a small failure. You should make them understand that one emerges as a stronger person after undergoing hardships.

OOO

What Not to Do

Inappropriate Behaviour of the Parents

1. Laughing at Inappropriate Behaviour

I was visiting my friend's house. Her baby son, aged one-and-a-half years, had just learnt to speak simple two-word sentences. Eager to show off her son's vocabulary, she would ask him a simple question and he would answer. The baby talk was very amusing. She asked him, "How does Papa show his anger?" The baby rattled off with eight-ten abuses. The parents burst out laughing and looked on proudly. No doubt, foul language did not seem foul from an innocent baby's mouth, but one day for sure, the same parents would take offence from his language.

Laughing or smiling at some action is a form of encouragement. When a child sees that his behaviour is pleasing to the parent, he repeats it to gain their approval. Inappropriate behaviour is reinforced, as in this case. This may lead to habit formation.

First, it was wrong on the part of the father to use bad language in front of the child, and second, the child should have been discouraged when he had mouthed bad words.

2. Subjecting to Solitary Confinement

Some people threaten and some even shut the child in a storeroom. These rooms are usually small, dark, suffocating and frightening. Shutting the child in such unfamiliar surroundings can leave a damaging effect on him. He may feel scared, uncomfortable or claustrophobic in the limited space. Instead of thinking about his inappropriate behaviour, he will think how he can escape from there. It can also cause lasting psychological trauma on the child's mind, like nightmares.

Once, tired of my two-year-old son's non-stop noise making capacity, I shut him in the bathroom intending to keep him there for 10-15 minutes, till he regretted his behaviour. I could hear him playing with the latch, without any hint of feeling sorry. After 10 minutes, I asked him if he was sorry and was ready to come out. He had succeeded in putting the latch on, from the inside. Now it was my turn to get worried. I shouted instructions from the ventilator on how he could unbolt it. He tried hard, but could not unlatch it. Thirty minutes had passed, and now I was getting panicky.

Luckily, my husband arrived. Standing on a stool with a twisted length of wire through the ventilator, he managed to open the lock. My son emerged unflustered, after his forty-minute ordeal. It was I who had suffered the agony. I would advise seriously against any kind of 'locking in'.

This technique is especially not advisable for children under two, as they might sustain some physical injury. It is better to use the 'time-out' technique for gross inappropriate behaviour. Banning the child from his favourite activity would serve as a better punishment for, him, for example, switching off the television, or not allowing him to go out and play with his friends would certainly act as a deterrent and discourage the child from behaving insolently.

3. Too Many Taskmasters

The screaming and shouting used to start in our neighbour's house at 5.30 a.m. From the noise you could make out that the father was telling his son to get up and start studying. When the boy did not wake up, he was threatened and abused. After 8.30 a.m. the mother's voice could be heard telling the boy to stop fooling around and concentrate on his work. It was the turn of the elder sister to take over the scolding and spanking job in the afternoons. In the evening, a tutor gave the boy lessons. This was followed by intermittent scolding sessions by the mother again and his father took over at night.

I found that the son was to appear for the board exams after three months. He was kept in the grindstone for 14 hours a day. The boy was over-aged and was kept under constant supervision. Even if he lifted his head or wanted to take a walk in the balcony, he was shouted at. After a few days, I could hear the boy screaming back at his parents. These shouting matches continued for three months. By that time, everybody in the neighbourhood knew that he was to appear for the board exams. He scored average marks. The yelling and shouting stopped and the neighbours heaved a sigh of relief.

Being told to study, almost perpetually by his parents, his sister and the tutor, lowered the child's self-esteem. He was made to feel as if he was careless and irresponsible. He was being scolded constantly by too many people. After sometime, the boy not only became immune to all the insults, but also started answering back defiantly. He had started to rebel.

By the manner his family treated him, the boy felt he was good for nothing. His self-esteem had touched rock-bottom. Shouting did not help in improving his performance. Had he been made to feel responsible for his own behaviour, he may have fared better. A single person could have supervised his work. The boy should have been made aware of the consequences, if he did not study. Though his parents had his best interests in mind, they ended up doing more harm than good. The manner they adopted was not right.

4. Insulting a Child Before His Peers

As the child steps into his teens, he may be spending more time with his peers than with his parents. Friends like to dress, talk, eat or behave alike. They like to share their problems and feelings. At this age a teenager feels that his friends understand him better than his parents.

Anju's son, Dhruv, had just come home after playing with his friends. He wanted to show his new music system to his friends. Anju started off, "I told you to return home by 7 p.m. See how dirty you look. Did you roll in mud? Your room is like a pigsty. All your dirty clothes are scattered on the floor. You never do what I tell you." To top it all, she said, "Your friends are no better, they set a bad example before you," adding insult to injury. Dhruv felt deeply insulted before his friends. He felt that he couldn't face them again. A feeling of low self-esteem had engulfed him.

Disciplining is a private matter. Time and place should be observed before rebuking a child. It is best to deal with him when he is alone and paying full attention to you.

5. Excessive Dependence on Hired Help

Sometimes we can have too much of a good thing. An army of servants may be attending on the little child. There is a maid to attend to the child's personal needs. A governess to supervise his studies and recreation. A driver to take him to school and back. The parents may feel that they have done very well for the child, that their responsibility ends here, and they are free to attend to their own official and social responsibilities.

Can a hired help provide the kind of environment which is conducive to good personality development? In such a situation a child feels neglected, in spite of having many people around. He longs for the love and affection of his parents. He feels that they do not care for him.

The maids or servants might use foul and obscene language. They may also have bad habits and manners. The child is very likely to copy them. They may also intimidate the child into doing what they want. A look at how maids deal with their respective wards in the park can be an eye-opener. After she has enjoyed the cheese sandwiches meant for the child, you could hear something like, "If you reveal this at home, I will beat the pulp out of you!"

No one can take the place of parents. It is only while the child is with his parents that he feels secure and emotionally satisfied.

Parents need to deliberately take some time out from their busy schedules. Otherwise, a time will come when he learns to live alone and would not need his parents!

6. Threats that are not Backed Up

Threats should only be made occasionally. They should be made only if the threat is fair and realistic, and you are willing to carry it out. For example, "If you do not finish your milk in time, I won't take you to the park" or "If you do not keep your new car in the cupboard, I will give it to someone else."

Do not make false threats to the child which you do not intend to carry out. The child is quick to recognise a hollow threat. My two-and-a-half-year-old daughter had an annoying habit of throwing different articles around the house: cutlery, shoes, clothes or whatever suited her fancy. I had to make at least three trips at different times during the day, to pick up all the stuff. Exasperated, one day I said, "I am going to throw you down the balcony along with the stuff you throw down." She thought about it for a minute and then, without hesitation, issued me a challenge, "Throw me down, Mummy!" I was dumbstruck. The young child had recognised that I would certainly not carry out my threat. She was so precious to me.

Sometimes the threats used by parents carry confused messages. A 'no' can turn into a 'maybe' or a 'yes'. I had told my son that he could not bring his friends in our drawing room to play any indoor game. If he wanted he could play with them in his own room. If he messed up any other room I would tell his friends to go.

One day while I was in the kitchen, I heard my son bring his group of grubby friends into the drawing room. He told his friends, "We can all play dark room, hide and seek here, nobody is going to scold us. My mother just threatens but she'll not throw us out." He had recognised weak authority.

Threaten if you must, but be sure to carry it out if the child persists. Next time you will not face the same problem.

7. Labelling a Child

"There are no 'problem children', there are only 'problem parents'." The saying seems apt many a time. Sometimes we unknowingly hurt a child's feelings. We slot him into categories, fixing a label upon him. He may be difficult or slow, stubborn or clumsy. And unconsciously, we start labelling him or his actions. We may say, "You are a very stubborn child. Why don't you put your video game away and study?" At other times we may say, "You really are clumsy, look at the way you are carrying glasses in the tray. You are sure to drop them." If they are frequently addressed to him, they are bound to affect his self-esteem or make him angry and stubborn.

While talking to a child, it is best to speak slowly and choose one's words carefully. If he feels that you are being rude to him, he will feel hurt and angry and could turn defensive and rebellious. It would be better to say, "According to the timetable, it is time for you to study", or, "Be more careful while carrying the tray", rather than slot him as stubborn or clumsy.

8. Adverse Stimuli Increases Aggression

A child is bound to be aggressive if he is raised in a chaotic environment. If he sees the family members hitting, disapproving, ignoring, and teasing habitually, he is likely to behave in a similar manner.

Aggression at any level can lead to a chain reaction. One is often bombarded with images and visuals from TV and other such media; the boss shouting at his employee, the employee screaming at his wife, the wife unleashing her anger on the adolescent, he in turn hitting his school-going brother, and the brother pinching the infant. This is indeed true of day-to-day life.

Living in cramped quarters with quarrelsome neighbours, landlords or local goons contributes to adverse surroundings.

Watching films or soap operas full of violence, hatred, bloodshed or sex has a lasting impact on a child's mind. Horror books can have similar effects. Studies show a positive correlation between aggression as seen on TV and the child's behaviour. You must monitor the quality of content that he is viewing. Try to make him watch programmes on channels like Discovery, ESPN, National Geographic and so on. Even watching the Cartoon Network is better than watching 'WWF'!

9. Starvation Technique

"If you cannot behave properly, better leave the dining table and go to your room. I am sure missing a meal will improve your manners tremendously." The child may sometimes walk away defiantly to his room. This kind of punishment is totally outdated and uncalled for. Food is the basic requirement and need. It is not a privilege. We can withdraw a privilege if the child exhibits inappropriate behaviour, but we cannot and should never tamper with his basic needs.

When the child goes to his room, just think about his feelings. Is he feeling hungry and miserable or is he feeling sorry? When a person is hungry, can he think about his own behaviour and accept his mistake? Even if you relent and call him back for dinner, your rebuke would sound ineffective.

A sensible way out is to tell the child about the consequences of his actions and carry them out. "Aditi, if you don't finish your dinner, you will not get any ice-cream", or "If you don't do that, I will not make any French fries for you."

10. Inconsistency in Behaviour

When we have established some ground rules with our children, we must try and stick to them as far as possible. We should not change them to suit our own convenience. For example, you have a rule that all children must come back home from the park by 7 o'clock. At seven, your friend drops in and you get busy chatting with her. When the children come home you may say, "Go and play for a little more time in the park, and don't disturb me for a while." In such a situation, the children begin to think that the rule is flexible. Don't expect them to adhere to this rule strictly henceforth. Try to be consistent in what you say and how you act.

Always try to exhibit the same reaction to similar behaviour, otherwise the child gets mixed messages. A child imitates an elderly relative and you laugh at his actions. Next time when he does it again in public, you scold him. When you laughed earlier, it was a sign of encouragement. Now you cannot condemn him for the same action.

11. Instant Gratification of All Demands

The desire to have more is insatiable. It is inherent in human nature. More is not necessarily better. Some parents comply with all the demands of the child, at once. They are financially well endowed and see no reason why they should not indulge the child. The child just has to wish for something and the doting parents or grandparents rush to fulfil it.

The child feels that he can have anything he likes, so his demands increase. If a child's demands are met very easily, he will not value them. Later, when a demand is not met, he might throw tantrums. An indulged child does not get along well with his peers because he wants everything to go his way.

A child has to be taught self-control and responsibility. He has to be motivated with rewards to behave well. A child who works hard to obtain something that he had asked for will treasure it more and make better use of it, as compared to a child who just demanded and got it.

12. Avoid Sarcasm

It is best to tell the child to stop behaving badly, in a straightforward, positive way rather than lacing it with sarcasm or a taunt. Cruel or sarcastic remarks should always be avoided. Children are quite sensitive, especially about their physical appearance. Comments referring to excessive weight, braces, pimples, complexion, height, etc. should never be made. You may remark, "Walking at that slow pace is not going to rid you of that ugly fat tyre around your middle, and stop eating those chips." Instead, it will be better to say, "I am sure you know that chips are rich in calories, try to avoid them. You will have to exercise more rigorously to burn off those calories."

Divya's daughter Ria, aged thirteen years, was overweight. She was quite lazy and loved eating fried food. Divya tried to force Ria many times either to exercise or cut down upon her diet of fried foods, but to no avail. Even scolding Ria did not produce any result. Ria paid no heed. Then, Divya tried a new approach. She bought some smart western clothes for Ria and explained to her that she would have to lose weight if she wanted to get into those smart, trendy clothes.

Ria was quite motivated. Nowadays, every teenager wants to appear slim and smart, so she started exercising daily, cut down on her fried food and was soon able to lose weight.

Sarcasm is lost on the little ones and is stinging in adolescence. Don't insult the child into doing something like household chores. The aim is to encourage him to do things on his own. It is better to say, "Polish your shoes for school tomorrow" rather than "When was the last time you polished your shoes? They are looking worse than a beggar's!"

Don't crack jokes that hurt a child's sensibilities. "I don't think your grades can go any lower than this. You must have set a new record for the lowest marks at school!" Remarks like these will never work. They just lower the child's self-esteem and morale.

13. Goading with Guilt or Fear

Sometimes we feel that instilling fear in a child is the easiest way of disciplining him. We may scare him with imaginary ghosts, robbers or animals. "Finish your meal fast, otherwise the wolf will come and carry you away." This may get results initially or temporarily, but it will not work in the long run. In time, the child will get wiser and call your bluff, or the fear may have a permanent impact on his mind. He may grow afraid of being alone, or of the dark, because he fears the wolf will come for him.

Similarly, instilling a feeling of guilt is also not a healthy technique. A guilt-ridden child may show poor performance in work and play. He will keep thinking about the consequence of his actions. "You are a bad boy, you made so much noise throughout the afternoon. Mummy had a nasty headache, now she has fallen sick. It is all because of you." This would not serve any purpose. It is far better to tell him to stop making noise, as it is very disturbing.

14. Continuous Nagging

As I entered my friend's house, I heard her son remark to his friends, "Yaar, don't be bothered by my mother's remarks, she is like a non-stop nagging machine and always talks in a loud tone." His rude remark startled me, but I found that it was indeed true. She started by criticising his hairstyle, way of walking, dressing sense, mode of speech, academic performance and ended at the disorder in his room. Continuous criticism can make the child stubborn and immune.

Constant nagging or criticism can turn the house into a battlefield. The mother should have picked up one problem that was bothering her the most, like poor performance at studies, and should have worked on it till it was corrected. In short, one should speak to children in a calm, non-threatening manner. Co-operate with them and try to sort out their problems. When one problem gets solved, it is time to work on the next one. The child is not a puppet, who will move mechanically as and when you pull the strings. Try to understand his feelings and lead him gently.

15. Difference in Opinion in Front of the Child

Difference in opinion about the child's behaviour should not be shown in front of him. The child feels confused and might also take advantage of it and have his way. He can choose to obey only those rules that suit him.

Here's what typically happens in a joint family. If the mother scolds the child for spilling his milk, the child rushes to sulk in his Dadi's arm, who consoles him. And, if the grandmother frowns at him for using bad language, the mother pets him.

When one person is handling a particular issue, he alone should exercise complete control, with no interference from any other family member. No one else should pet or sympathise with him at this stage. If the child is behaving in an ill-mannered way with one family member today and gets encouraged, the next day he may behave in the same way with you.

You should always support your spouse's stand before a child. The decision taken to handle the problem situation should be a joint one. You can discuss the problem with your partner when you both are alone. You should present a united front with a common stand before the child. Take the case of your fifteen-year-old daughter, who wants to go for a party to her friend's house and stay overnight. The father does not want the girl to go because he feels that she is not mature enough to take care of herself. But you feel that she may become the odd one out in her group. Both of you can discuss the pros and cons and can arrive at a joint decision. The teenager can go to the party but her father will pick her up at 10.30 p.m. sharp. Tell her in advance that you both will think about it and give your decision. If the child comes to know that both the parents are having a difference of opinion, she might try to manipulate the situation. She may say, "Mama is ready but you have to have your way, don't you!" or something like "Papa, please say yes, Mama will surely agree then."

This way the child respects and loves both the parents instead of classifying them as "kind, strong, weak, lenient, authoritarian", and disciplining is made easier.

OOO

Avoiding
Conflicts

Simple Ways to Avoid Turning a Home into a Battlefield

1. Ignoring Temper Tantrums

A two-year-old cousin of mine, Pallavi, had mastered the art of throwing tantrums. When she could not have it her way, she would hit her little fists on the ground and wall. Alternatively, she would bang her head on the wall. Scared by this, my aunt would rush to placate her. Her tantrums increased, especially at market places or at eating joints. Her mother would feel embarrassed by the look of curious onlookers, and would give in to her wishes.

Advised by my mother, my aunt started ignoring her tantrums. If in a shop, she would look the other way or walk out of the shop. If at home, she would calmly go to another room, switch on the TV and relax. When Pallavi saw that no one was paying any heed to her, her tantrums subsided, continuing at a milder rate. She also started feeling a little insecure because her mother was not paying her the sort of attention that she was used to. Slowly, her tantrums declined and finally disappeared altogether.

So, the best way to treat a tantrum is to ignore it altogether.

2. Using Imagination

Children sometimes have fixed ideas or notions about certain things. If something does not match their conception, they may just reject it or create a scene.

67

I had put tomatoes and cheese on bread and baked it, for a quick snack. My two-and-a-half-year-old loved pizzas, but refused to eat that sandwich insisting that pizzas were always round and never rectangular. I had either to prepare a new snack or force him to eat it. My five-year-old solved the problem. He whispered to me, "Mom, why don't you cut the corners of the bread, shaping it round like the pizza, and then bake it? I am sure bhaiya will like it." The little one feasted on the 'round' pizzas.

A little imagination at times can work wonders. A friend of mine wanted her bathroom tiles to be cleaned in the summer months. Nobody volunteered to help. She made her two sons, who were six and eight years old, wear swimsuits and announced, "The water games are about to begin. Pulkit is given a sponge to clean this wall and Anubhav is given that wall. You can splash, jump or dance (the shower could be used). Let's see whose wall is the cleanest!" Music was put on, and I am sure the kids enjoyed themselves thoroughly.

3. Using Distractions

Young children have short attention spans. They can be easily distracted. If they are about to do something that you don't want them to, shift the focus. Increase the possibility of experiencing a positive emotion. Try to engage them in an enjoyable activity. Use a warm, friendly voice so that they are attracted towards you.

A one-year-old has laid his hands on your diary and wants to tear it. You distract him by saying, "Look at this lovely red car, there it goes!"

A three-year-old is throwing a tantrum. You can say, "I am going to the market, does anyone want to come with me?" or, "I am going to prepare hot popcorns in the kitchen, do you want to help?"

A big fight between the siblings can be stopped by remarking, "What a lovely cartoon film they are showing on the TV. Jerry is beating Tom to pulp." Or, "Look what Papa has brought from the market!"

4. Have a Contest

"I think I had an easier time raising six kids together, compared to two children of the present generation," my mother-in-law often remarks. "Children in our days knew how to share and care. I had three boys and three girls in the house. The chores were equally divided. We were always having contests among the children to encourage them. Sometimes we had a contest on who could roll out the roundest and softest chapati, with their father as the judge, or which group would make the best vegetable soup and so on. We even organised a competition as to who would polish his part of the car best. It turned out to be more a game than a chore."

A contest entails that a child develops a spirit of healthy competition. Sometimes he may do a task readily which he is otherwise reluctant to do. Winning a contest gives him a high and encourages him to perform better.

This trick can be used with siblings. One can get them into the contest mood with things like – who will finish his dinner faster or pack his bag first and so on. This can also be employed with a single child. You can make him compete against time or yourself. You can say, "I am going to count till ten, you have to finish your milk. Let's see who wins." Or, "Let us see if you can learn words for your dictation within twenty minutes." Remember to give the child ample time to complete the activity. Let him win most of the time to encourage him.

5. Substitution

My two-and-a-half-year-old daughter had just learnt to hold a crayon. When I was in the kitchen or working elsewhere, she would exercise her imagination on the drawing room walls. I gave her innumerable drawing books and diaries to scribble on, but she enjoyed writing on the walls. Finally, I got her a blackboard roll with plenty of coloured chalks. I hung the blackboard in her playroom. She enjoyed herself immensely.

If a child is doing something which is not correct, give him something to do which is correct. Children have to be taught how, when and where to do certain things. Learn to find quick, inexpensive, attention-grasping substitutes, which can be used with the child.

My friend's son, Rohan, used his mother's expensive lipsticks, creams and eyebrow pencils to paint his face as a 'Red Indian', a dacoit or a 'dada', every afternoon. She got him a box of non-toxic face paints, which could be easily washed. He is happy, giving his face a new look everyday.

6. Ignoring Small Mistakes

Sometimes it is best to ignore small mistakes. A child, while playing, may just repeat some foul language he heard from somewhere, without knowing its meaning. Do not pay any attention to him. He will soon forget it. However, if you pounce upon him and ask him to say sorry, he may repeat it after a while to see its effect on other people.

Similarly, if a child unconsciously touches his genital area in public, ignore it. If he continues, however, corrective action could be taken. Children sometimes simply outgrow some actions. Give them space.

7. Animating Objects

Sometimes children knowingly or unknowingly spoil, destroy, break, mutilate objects or other living things. Sometimes they vent their anger by throwing their toys or stamping on them. They may crush plants and flowers and want to throw small stones at dogs and cats. They have to be taught to respect living beings and their property. An easy and effective way to deal with the situation is to animate objects.

If a child throws a favourite doll in a corner, the parent can mimic a child's voice (supposedly the imaginary voice of the doll) and say, "Mini, you have hurt me. My hand is aching. I will not stay in your house now and am going to your friend's house." Chances are that the child will be surprised, and will probably laugh and rush to pick up the doll in her arms.

You can apply this wonderful way in a number of ways. "Raju, I am a living being, you are crushing my leaves. How will I live now?" Raju will definitely take notice of this. The same trick can be used to give a positive output to the child. The plant can say, "I love it when you water me Raju. My leaves look so fresh and green. I'll grow some pretty flowers for you." Small children love this world of fantasy and make-believe.

8. Change the Environment

Sometimes many behavioural problems do not require shouting or even a discussion. A simple change in environment can solve the problems.

Toddlers love to play with the family phone, the cosmetics on the dressing table, the keys or the medicines in the drawers or the TV remote. As soon as the baby begins to crawl, it is best to shift such things. Keep the phone at a higher place, the cosmetics inside the dressing table, the medicines in the topmost drawer and the remote below the cushion. Change their places again if the child discovers them. If he doesn't see them, he won't be tempted to play with them.

Children like the informal atmosphere of the park, gardens, and swings, where they do not have to listen to the dos and don'ts. It is not fair to expect a child to sit stiffly, putting on his best behaviour for great lengths of time in hotels or theatres. Avoid taking them to such places. They may create a scene there. Take them to fun food joints and amusement parks. Watch them enjoy themselves.

9. Pretence-playacting

Sometimes the child realises his mistake, if it is put forward in a light way. Pretence-playacting is a useful trick to show a child how he behaves in a certain situation.

An eight-year-old-boy, I know, takes hours to finish his home assignment. His mother sits patiently with him guiding and supervising him. He gives feeble excuses, "I am having a headache", "My fingers are aching", "I am tired", "I feel weak", and so on.

One day the mother decided to enact a small play. She acted as the boy and the boy acted as the mother, supervising her, like she did. She pretended to do the homework, making a hundred and one excuses for not working properly. The child reprimanded her and told her to hurry. She persisted with her situation as a demonstration of his very behaviour. Of course, his speed improved considerably after this one-act play.

10. Use Humour to Diffuse the Situation

Sometimes, a tense situation can be diffused when children join in the fun and stop behaving badly.

One day my friend's fifteen-year-old son was troubling his twelve-year-old brother. Despite being given a verbal warning he continued to rag the youngster. My friend used her most authoritative voice and said, "I, the great empress of Hindustan, have spied a big monster in my empire. He is troubling my subjects. I command that he be captured and thrown to the crocodiles. He has just one chance of escape if he begs forgiveness." The elder son, in the spirit of play, bowed before my friend and said, "Your Majesty! Do forgive me, I am scared of crocodiles."

Similarly, one day my ten-year-old son was kicking and hitting his sister. After a while, she gave it back as good as she got. I took a glass as a make-believe mike and started off, "The fight between Muscle-man and Big-chi continues. Muscle-man has landed a mighty kick on Big-chi. Big-chi has managed a solid punch on Muscle-man's face. Both are going strong. Anybody wants ring side seats? Who wants to bet on Muscle-man?" Both the children burst out laughing.

Sometimes, it is good to lose your inhibitions and be a kid yourself. You don't have to be perfect all the time. Create situations in which children can laugh, act, talk in a silly, spontaneous way. Do the ridiculous and unexpected. Try to sing and dance with children. Watch them laugh with you.

11. Hold the Child

This technique is for infants, toddlers and pre-school kids. When the child refuses to listen to your verbal commands and you feel that he may harm himself, it is the time to hold him.

For instance, a toddler is very fond of poking his fingers in plug sockets. (You may have plugged all the sockets in your house with dummy plugs, but trust him to find one, which is open). Telling him verbally to stop does not have any effect. It is better that you pick him up and hold him firmly for some time. The same is to be done when the toddler wants to climb down the stairs on his own or rushes out to fondle a stray dog.

While holding the child, see that it does not do him any physical harm, e.g. holding the wrists or shoulder so tightly that bruises appear or he experiences pain. The child should be able to breathe properly. At the same time, try to calm the excited child. You may have to hold the child for 10-15 minutes, so that he forgets what he was doing. On the other hand, sometimes the infant may run back to the same spot and do the same thing again. He may keep looking back to see if he is being observed. He is testing you. Be ready to hold him again.

Children are born explorers. They are full of curiosity and observe all new actions and things. This technique is specially useful if the parents feel that the child faces some potential harm, like when he is running across a busy street, touching a hot iron, catching crawling insects, or putting dirty things in the mouth and the like.

This method can be used sometimes when the child shows or behaves badly outdoors, say in a restaurant or a shop. If he drops cutlery on the floor, bangs the spoon against the plate, puts the salt-cellar in his mouth or pulls at the tablecloth, hold him in your arms and remove all the distracting articles from his hands. When he calms down, ask for an infant chair for him so that he cannot touch anything on the table.

The child should not suffer any pain. He should only feel the firmness of your resolve.

Effective Dealing
with the Child

Improving Communication with the Child

1. Patience Pays

Try to remain patient and cool under adverse circumstances. Usually, it's easier said than done. Sometimes, a child may behave unbecomingly, just to test your patience. Do not react instantly. The situation is likely to remain the same after some time, only now you may be able to handle it better, after giving it a thought.

Remember to count upto ten before taking any action. If you are angry, it's better to count to twenty. The time gap between the moments when you are about to act, being acutely aware of the problem and counting those moments, enables you to increase your perspective, cool down and act in a rational manner.

Patience is required in abundance at certain times. You start toilet-training your child when he is one or one-and a-half-years old. When he indicates in time that he wants to go to the toilet, praise him. When he does not give any indication, ignore it. Patience is sure to pay dividends. By the time he goes to play school he is bound to be toilet-trained.

2. Have a Heart-to-Heart Talk

It is imperative to reserve some time exclusively for every child. It can be half-an-hour once or twice a week. This is the time to have a heart-to-heart talk with the child about his school, friends, games, teachers or whatever topic he wants to discuss.

Many times we try to do more than one thing at a time, in order to save time, like using the cordless phone, checking on the washing machine, answering the doorbell, chopping the vegetables or reading the newspaper while talking to children. This does not coordinate well with them. We may be physically present for the child, but our minds are elsewhere.

When we do too many things, it becomes impossible to concentrate on the present moment. We become less focussed and effective. It is best to focus on the child exclusively, and listen attentively to what he has to say.

Talk to the child about his needs, friends, problems, ambitions, and activities at school. Make him feel that you are genuinely interested in him. Sometimes simply talking can solve quite a few problems. Suggest a gentle solution, if it is possible. Encourage him to tackle the problem himself. A boy pretended to have stomachache every morning, so that he did not have to go to school. In the evening, he was perfectly normal. Talks with him revealed that senior students at school were bullying him. A talk with the teachers solved the problem.

These talks are especially necessary with adolescents. She or he may be experiencing some anxieties related to the physical changes in her or his body, peer pressure, scholastic pressure, fear of excessive competition, growing sexual needs, attraction of the opposite sex, experimentation with smoking, drugs or alcohol and so on. A parent should reassure the child that all this is normal. All these anxieties are expected at this age. This can help relieve undue pressures off the adolescent mind.

You can also warn him/her about the dangers of experimentation.

A healthy talk ensures that many problems are solved by mere exchange of words.

3. Giving Reasons for Restrictions

As children grow older, they want to know the reason behind each and every action. In most cases, a good reason can satisfy them. The rhyme and reason for restrictions and limitations can be given in clear and simple terms.

My six-year-old sister was very fond of dressing up. She would take out jewellery from my mother's closet in the afternoon, wear each piece and admire herself in the mirror. The jewellery was expensive and delicate. One day my mother made her sit next to her. She showed her how each piece should be arranged on the velvet case. "I have kept all these pieces safely because I want to give them to you when you grow up. Rough handling will spoil the delicate setting." My sister understood immediately.

"I don't want you to have so many chocolate biscuits before dinner because then you will not be able to have your dinner. Take only two." A remark like this can stop an eleven-year-old from finishing the whole pack. This method works very well with teenagers. You can say, "I want you to be home by 8.30 p.m. from the birthday party. I am worried about your safety and will not sleep till you return."

4. Use a Firm Tone

A firm 'no', without raising your voice, is a good way of showing disapproval. Even infants as old as 9-10 months can understand this command. This technique can be used effectively when we sense some physical danger for the child or when he behaves improperly. For example, when the infant is about to touch a hot iron, or follow someone down the staircase or tries to pet a stray dog, this can be effectively employed.

The body language should be consistent with the command to show that you mean business. Look at the child, stand straight with a stern expression and call out his name. You can move your finger from side-to-side, indicating 'no'. Or perhaps, point, clap or snap your fingers. The command should be loud and clear.

If the body language is weak or mild, the child may continue with whatever he is doing. For instance, if a seven-year-old boy is hitting his three-year-old sister, he might not stop if you tell him to 'cut it out', while casually reclining on a sofa. He is getting a mixed message, which is indirect and confusing. You have to tell him to 'stop it' in a firm no-nonsense voice.

Children who are sensitive can sense parental disapproval by the mere narrowing of eyes or lifting of the eyebrows.

5. Give Specific Commands

A child is able to comprehend specific commands easily as compared to general or vague commands. 'Do not trouble me', 'Behave yourself', 'Control yourself', 'Do not act stupid', 'Do not make me mad', 'Stop playing like a fool', are all vague commands. A child may not understand what is required of him.

Some specific commands can be:

Infants

1. No, don't touch it.
2. No, don't run, sit, etc.

80

Pre-school Children

1. Stop drumming on the table at once.
2. Close the tap at once.
3. Stop hitting her.

School-going Children

1. Pick up all the torn paper pieces from the floor.
2. Switch off the TV at once.
3. Stop the noise immediately.

Adolescents

1. Do not lie on the sofa.
2. Use the phone only when necessary.
3. Put away your sports equipment after using it.

If specific commands are given, children will not have any excuse for not doing what is told.

6. Talk in a Calm Manner

Talking or communicating is a vital part of the disciplining procedure. Use words that reflect honesty, respect and sensitivity. The child is more likely to cooperate with you, if handled gently. Do not shut doors, for example, don't say, "No, I don't want to hear any excuses", "That is final, I don't want any further discussions", "Don't make me angry". The key to cooperation from the child is to leave the door open.

Speak to him in a calm, non-threatening way. Speak to him as you would like to be spoken to. Avoid verbal put-downs. 'I' sentences will prove to be more effective as compared to 'you' sentences. By this method, you tell the child how his behaviour is troubling you and how unhappy you are with the present situation.

Use Short, Simple Sentences with Infants

I like this, I don't like this, I want this, and so on.

Pre-school Children

Aryan had scribbled on the wall. Instead of scolding him, his mother remarked, "I was very upset when I saw your bedroom walls today. You have scribbled on them with your crayons. Since the walls are washable I want you to take a wet cloth and remove the marks and stains." After he had cleaned the walls, she had to work hard on it again, but the child realised that he had committed a mistake and would not repeat it.

School-going Children

Garima's mother told her, "I am afraid that some of your expensive doll furniture is going to be damaged or lost, as you have scattered it carelessly in the room. Pick it up and arrange it in the dollhouse neatly."

Adolescents

Dhruv's father firmly told him, "Yesterday I was very upset when the neighbours complained about the loud volume of your stereo deck. Music is of course very pleasing, but it should not disturb others. I am sure you will play it at a low volume in future."

7. Listen to the Child

Many a time our children want to tell us something. It may be an experience at school or an incident at the playfield. Sometimes we are too tired or busy or stressed out to even listen to them. We may say impatiently, "Later, tell me later." Sometimes we do listen, but our minds are elsewhere. We may just nod with an occasional 'aha' or 'really'. Listening attentively to a child is very important, for it sometimes gives us a clue as to why he is behaving badly or doing what he is doing.

Try this. Take the child (infant) in your lap or sit close to him. Both should be comfortable. Make an eye-to-eye contact with the child. Listen to what he has to say. Do not interrupt him and pay total attention to what he says. Make appropriate responses to show that you are listening actively, like 'go on', 'wow', 'really'. Gather information and learn the truth about your child. You can ask some questions to clarify doubts later.

Your well-behaved three-year-old child has suddenly taken to using abusive language. You are at a loss as to how and from where he has picked up this bad habit, as nobody in your house uses foul language. One day he says, confiding in you, "Mama, Varun is bad, when we play, he uses bad words." You can talk to him and tell him why he should not use such language.

You note that your school-going daughter is reluctant to go to school everyday. Casual talks with her reveal that her friends are teasing her about her pimples. It is time to tell her about the way hormones function and how it is all a part of growing up.

Your adolescent child has been acting in a sullen, irritated way for a week. Talks with him may reveal the root cause of his problem. "Mama, I did not join my friends who were burning crackers in the school. Now, no one in my group is talking to me. They are calling me a coward." It is time to tell him the difference between real bravery and tomfoolery.

8. Family Meetings Help

'A family that eats together and prays together, stays together' is the point being emphasised upon in the Indian films these days. The most important point to be noted here is that the family members who communicate with each other, stick together. Does it really help in holding family meetings? Definitely. A weekly or fortnightly meeting to discuss family plans, outing, goals or problems is of immense help. Half an hour can be set aside on a Friday evening or a Saturday afternoon when all the members are in a relaxed mood after a hectic week. All the members have to keep this time slot free.

Some ground rules can be established before the meeting starts:

- Each member gets a turn to speak without interruption.
- He can voice his problems, difficulties or plans.
- No screaming or yelling at each other is allowed.
- No distractions like TV or video games are allowed at this time.
- Parents or the elders are the final judges.

For instance, let's take a look at this problem. Rahul, aged fourteen, shares a room with Rohan, aged twelve. Both have constant fights on some issue or the other.

- Rahul is an ardent movie buff and wants to put pin-ups of his favourite stars in the room. Rohan wants to decorate the walls with posters of the cricketing legends.
- Rahul cannot work till he hears music and Rohit can work in absolute silence only.
- Rahul can study only during the late night hours while Rohit cannot sleep with the lights on.
- Both use the room but none is bothered about its cleanliness or tidiness.

- Rohit likes to use Rahul's things but does not keep them back at their proper place.

It is evident that some rules have to be laid down so that Rahul and Rohit share the room peacefully. These rules can be put in writing and pasted on the bathroom door.

- Rohit has been allotted the right hand side wall of the room and Rahul the left one. They can decorate them as they like with posters or pictures of their choice.

- Rahul has to use headphones to listen to music, if Rohit is studying in the room.

- Rahul can either use a table lamp or study in the living room, if Rohit is about to sleep.

- Rohit has to take Rahul's permission before borrowing anything. He has to return it safely and keep it at its proper place.

- Both the children are jointly responsible for keeping the room tidy. Both can take turns.

- Each one will make his bed and keep his desk clean and tidy.

This is the time when family members compare notes. Children can be praised for their good behaviour, achievements in academics, sports and extra-curricular activities. Plans can be made for the coming weekends, vacations and other events. The meeting should be a relaxed and a positive experience for each family member.

9. Perceive the Difference

Studies have shown that any overt action of aggression tends to reduce the tendency to do other acts of aggression. That is, if an individual slams a door or kicks a chair, his anger towards other persons will be reduced. Parents have to learn to perceive the difference between socially acceptable and unacceptable behaviour of the children. Bashing up younger brothers or sisters will make him a bully but choosing a career with the Armed Forces will bring him laurels.

Sports like rifle shooting, boxing, wrestling, weightlifting, shot-put, javelin throw, archery and so on are socially acceptable sports which can satisfy the aggressive instinct.

Chores like working in the garden, washing the car, dusting carpets, hammering nails, etc. require physical strength. They can divert his mind from aggression and put him in a more reasonable frame of mind. These activities provide an outlet to the destructive feelings of the child.

10. Seek Professional Help

If you have struggled with a family problem, or a problem concerning your children, for a period of more than six months or a year and are still unable to find a workable solution, it is now the time to see a child counsellor or a family now the therapist.

Kritika, the ten-year-old daughter of an elite couple, had been scoring very poorly in school assessments and was behaving badly as well. She refused to answer questions put up by teachers. She bullied the children in her class. She fared poorly in sports and did not take part in any extra-curricular activity. Rewards, incentives, shouting and beating did not work. This continued for an entire year. The school teachers warned the parents that she would be detained in the same class and face serious disciplinary action.

Luckily her case was put up before the school counsellor. She studied her case history in detail. It came to light that Kritika's parents were not spending enough time with her. The father was busy with his business and the mother had to attend to the social obligations of a huge joint family. The only outings the child ever had were business parties. Her only means of entertainment and companionship was TV, with only the servants to supervise her. She neglected her homework and watched the never-ending soap operas. Her schoolwork suffered. Teachers at school reprimanded her. The other children laughed at her. Unable to bear the taunts, she bullied them. Because of her poor performance, she was detained in the lower class. She felt ridiculed and ashamed. She did not make any friends with the younger lot and tried to shut herself out from all activities.

The problem aggravated to huge proportions. The school counsellor advised a change in the environment for the child. Her class section was changed. The parents were counselled and told about the root cause of the problem. They were advised to spend more time with her. During summer break, she was to be given extra coaching so that she could catch up with her classmates. Her problem was discussed with the new class teacher. She was told not to punish her in front of her classmates.

The counsellor in this case was successful in bridging the ever-increasing gap between the child, the school and her parents. Counsellors can help a family find solutions to problems related to parent-child conflict, child behaviour and so on. They help in reducing family tensions by increasing the awareness and understanding of both parents and the child. They are able to view the perspective from both the child's angle and the parents'.

Sometimes a child is unable to talk freely or share his feelings with his parents. He may open up to a third person who is trained to deal with such situations. Take this advice and work on the problem.

Telling the Child
Consequences

Telling the Child the Outcome of his Behaviour

1. Immediate Reward Reinforces Good Behaviour

A reward encourages good behaviour and discourages bad behaviour. A reward can be a favourite snack, going for an outing, family picnic, watching a favourite cartoon show, a bed-time story or just a hug or a few words of praise. Immediate reward for good behaviour is a very effective technique for disciplining.

This works especially well with the little ones. "Finish your dinner quickly and I will tell you the story of 'Goldilocks'." When the child finishes his food, you must tell him the story. Remember, do not postpone it to another day. Immediate gratification leads to positive results and good behaviour.

The rewards have to vary. Some children get used to certain rewards and will not act without it. For instance, if a slab of chocolate is the reward for doing homework, it will not be completed till he is assured of the chocolate.

Words of praise or a hug work equally well. "Well done, you have arranged your books beautifully." After saying this, you pat his back or give a peck on the cheek. Believe me, it can work wonders. A delayed reward may break the association of stimulus and response and may become ineffective.

Praise is the best reward and it works wonders with children of any age group. Even a toddler recognises his mother's pleased smile and words of praise. Material reward should be used sparingly and with caution. Excessive usage may make them less effective. Praise may be given along with a material reward.

Always make sure that you are giving due weightage to good behaviour, so that it is repeated in future. You can say to your thirteen-year-old, "You have ironed your school uniform so well, I will prepare your favourite 'bhel puri' today."

'Cash rewards' are popular in the west. However, you can give small cash rewards for good behaviour occasionally. This may be collected in a piggy bank. Later, the money can be used to buy a favourite toy or sweets from the market.

Also make sure that you give equal praise to all the kids who have worked with you. For example, praising a boy for doing minor household chores, while expecting a girl to do it in a matter-of-fact manner should not be done.

2. Immediate Reprimand

Reprimanding immediately, instead of delaying it, will have more disciplinary value. Often the mother is so busy with her schedule that she does not even have time to discipline the children, or wants to pass on the task to her husband. She might say, "Switch off the TV and study for your test, or else I am going to complain to your father about your excessive TV viewing," from the kitchen. The child may just say, "Mummy, I am watching a cricket match, I want to see just two more overs." I can assure you that these 'two more overs' never finish. Later, he may get very little time to study for his test.

If the father comes home late, there is very little time for interaction and the child may escape without any disapproval. The father may be too tired or mentally exhausted to deal with the child. The child may also put up a 'show', making it appear that he had been working very hard throughout the day.

All the parents should agree on certain ground rules. The foremost is that the person who first witnesses inappropriate behaviour should deal with it. If we delay or dilly-dally, the child might think that the parent is weak and ineffective, and unable to function independently. The other parent is made out to be the 'bad guy' or the discipline enforcer. These extreme images are not good. Both parents should be equally effective in correcting their child's behaviour.

Never take away your partner's powers as a parent and never give away yours. Gone are the days when the father was the only disciplining authority.

I have heard a woman saying rather proudly, "My son doesn't listen to me at all. He is scared only of his Dad. He talks back to me all the time." Encouraging this kind of behaviour can lead to problems later on. The child will hold less respect for his mother.

A single parent has to give the problem a thoughtful and unbiased view. Make a decision and stick to it.

3. Make a Deal

Choose the most annoying habit of the child, which causes maximum arguments, and target it. It may be nail biting, getting low marks in the maths test (you know that he is capable of doing better) or an untidy mess in your adolescent's bedroom. Strike a deal.

Every Sunday examine both the hands of the child. See if they show signs of growth or appear bitten. For every unbitten nail, he gets a sum of, say, two rupees. He can get a maximum of twenty rupees per week. The child may get six rupees in the first week or ten rupees in the second week. I am sure he will start getting twenty rupees in about six months' time. Now wean him off the reward. Instead of rupees he can also be promised a small gift.

Similarly, if a child does five problem-sums from a reference book for five days in a week, he gets to decide the menu for Sunday lunch, or, you can take him out for dinner.

If a messy teenager cleans his room by a fixed time limit, you can allow him to go for a movie with his friends on Saturday.

4. Set Time Limits

It is a good idea to set clear time limits for work, play, entertainment and going out. The child should know that he has to adhere to a set schedule and what is expected of him. Children feel safe and comfortable when they do things in time.

Make it clear to him that the time limits are non-flexible. (If you give him an extra ten minutes for cricket, he will stretch it to half-an-hour). The time limits should be different for weekdays and weekends. On weekends, the entertainment time (TV, comics, video games, etc.) can be increased. During examination time, the time limits can be changed to suit the need of the hour.

Also, let the child face the consequences if he breaks the set time limits. For example, one hour of TV is permitted every day, and two-three hours on Sundays. If he watches TV for more time, he has to compensate it by cutting on/

forgoing his playtime and concentrating on his home assignments. This will make him watch selective programmes.

If your teenager comes late from a party by two hours, he has to forgo his next party.

5. Making Up

A child has to learn to make up for anything that has been lost, damaged, or taken away. He has to learn to make amends for impolite, rude or careless behaviour. He should learn to take responsibility for his deeds. He should know the consequences of his actions.

The simplest form of making up is realising your mistake and saying 'sorry', if you have been impolite or have misbehaved. The child should realise that 'sorry' is not just a lip movement, it should be spoken with a feeling that the same action will not be repeated again. Sometimes children find it difficult to say sorry. They can make up by shaking hands. My daughter has this cute habit of writing 'sorry' notes if she has misbehaved.

My five-year-old son lost his three-year-old cousin's 'Hot Wheels' car while playing. The little one burst into tears. My son offered his brand new car to him as a replacement. The little one was pacified. Luckily, the missing car was found a week later and an exchange was made. I felt proud of my son's decision.

Similarly, if a child has been rude to his mother, he can make up by doing an extra chore in the house, like weeding the garden or fixing his mother's favourite drink and so on.

6. Take Away a Privilege

Children look forward to many recreational activities over the weekend, like go-carting, paddle-boating, playing pool or video games.

When children repeatedly conduct themselves in an undesirable manner, some privileges can be taken away. For example, stop the weekend outings, if he is not finishing the home assignment in time and getting poor grades. Explain why his privilege is being taken away and when it is likely to be restored. Do not relent till he shows adequate improvement.

If a child watches TV in excess till late night hours, the cable network can be disconnected till he promises to limit the viewing time. While doing so, you may also have to make big/small sacrifices yourself, if you take such an action. But stick to your decision, if you want any improvement to take place.

7. Giving Time-out

If the child is behaving in an exceptionally destructive or aggressive way, like hitting a sibling or a parent, shouting, screaming or whining, he should be asked to sit in a corner without taking part in any conversation, games or activity. The child must just sit silently so as to make him realise his mistake. The period of isolation may vary from ten minutes to half-an-hour, depending on the age of the child. The child should feel sorry after the specified period. This method is especially useful for pre-schoolers and school-goers.

2-5 years: Ten to fifteen minutes on a stool or a baby chair in the corner of the room. (Do not let the child out of your sight as, in this mood, he might show inappropriate behaviour in the other room or outdoors. He might even open the main gate and walk on to the road.)

5-12 years: The child may be sent to his own room for 20-30 minutes. Time should be given to the child to regain control of his behaviour. Remember, going to his own room, reading comics, watching TV or playing with toys is not the idea of time-out. The child should be away from any kind of stimulation or distraction. Checking on the child after 15 minutes is a good idea.

This technique can be used effectively for teenagers also. They may be sent for time-out for longer periods. The time-out should be dull so that the teenager gets time for introspection.

Children may shout or scream during the time-out. Parents should not weaken their stand or lessen the stipulated time-out. Being lenient would weaken the impact of the punishment.

This method has to be used sometimes in public places or when you go visiting and the child behaves in a disobedient, destructive way. Take him out in the garden or to the footpath or ask him to go and sit in your vehicle. If the child resists, you may have to even physically carry him. Sit quietly with the child. After the time is over, talk to the child. If he promises to show better behaviour, he may be taken back to the place.

8. Confiscate Items Causing Problems

Many times a pre-schooler uses his bat, scissors, drumstick, baton, etc. to cause damage to property or people or even self. He should be shown its correct use by the parents or siblings. If the child persists in using this instrument in a destructive manner, the item should be hidden for a short period, say a day or two.

Explain to your child the reason for taking away the article. Tell him the time for which you will keep it. Explain how it hurts the other person or damages the article. Do not bow down before the child's crying if he demands the bat back. Be firm. When the time is over, hand over the article back to him with a warning. When the child uses the article properly, praise him.

School-children sometimes acquire the habit of throwing used chewing gum carelessly in the house. It can create havoc in the house, sticking to furniture, clothing and floor. My friend had to cut part of her daughter's hair to remove the stuck chewing gum. All chewing gums were confiscated, a ban was imposed on purchasing new ones till, after an interval, everybody promised its safe disposal.

Nowadays children have more temptations. They spend extra hours reading comics, playing video games, trump cards, etc. Mobile phones are more of a fashion statement rather than to be used at times of need. Phones are used to make blank or obscene calls. Computers are used widely, not for any assignments, but for chatting, playing games or maybe even watching pornographic stuff. If you feel that the article is being misused, give a warning. If it fails, it is best to confiscate the item or limit or restrict its use. Monitor the activities of the child closely. If you feel that he regrets his behaviour, release the article. If you feel that there is no change, it is time to extend the confiscation period. Slowly, the child will realise that you are serious about your word and he will make an effort to amend his habits.

9. Give Options

After watching the 'Kaun Banega Crorepati' show in India, I think even a three-year-old has come to know the meaning of an option. Giving a child an alternative or option makes him happier since he feels that he is making a decision.

Sometimes, a child does not go according to the parent's wishes because he just wants to assert his independence. One way to avoid conflict is by offering choices. These can be given in any kind of situation. Let the children do their own thinking and decision-making. They gain a healthy sense of power and self-esteem. At the same time, parents retain some control over the child's behaviour. This trick works for all age groups and is especially useful with the teenagers.

You can give the following options to the child:

Food

1. Would you like to take sandwiches or paranthas for your tiffin?
2. Would you like tomato juice or soup at dinner time?
3. Do you want to drink cold or hot milk with chocolate?

Clothes

1. Do you want to wear your blue dinner shorts or skirts?
2. Do you want to wear your pink or yellow dress to the party?
3. Would you like to keep your hair loose and attach clips or make a ponytail?

Outing and Entertainment

1. Would you like to go to the amusement park or the bowling alley?
2. Do you want to watch the cartoons or the magic show?

3. Would you like to visit Granny or Aunty this week?

Chores

1. Would you like to shell the peas or cut salad?
2. Would you like to help father in the garden or do a bit of dusting?
3. Will you tidy your room this Saturday or Sunday?

Once in a while this technique may misfire. My six-year-old, when given an option to have ice cream with mango cubes or tooti-frooti ice-cream, opted for having the first followed by the second later.

10. Fair's Fair

In this method, the child is given an opportunity to decide the consequence of his or her own inappropriate behaviour. The child accepts responsibility for his behaviour. He is given some time to think about his actions and then decide the punishment on his own and rectify the damage done.

A three-year-old child spills his soup on the floor. (It is a fairly common occurrence happening every alternate day.) He must get a mop and clean it. (You can clean it up again later).

A child sketches on the walls. He cleans the wall with sponge and soap.

A ten-year-old litters the room with paper while making his project. He collects every bit of paper and throws it into the dustbin.

A boy teases his younger sister and makes her cry. He plays her favourite game with her for half an hour.

A teenager has dirtied his socks excessively. He must wash them.

11. Using Natural Consequences

When a child misbehaves, show him the natural consequences of his misbehaving. If a child eats too many chocolates and does not brush his teeth regularly, he is bound to get cavities. Remind him of the time when he went to the dentist and saw a screaming youngster.

A child does not put away his carrom-board counters after a game with his friends. He is likely to lose them. As a result, he will not be able play the game next time as he will have incomplete counters.

If a child shows careless behaviour, try to point out its natural consequences. Sometimes, it works so well that there is no need for further action.

My daughter had to raise a small sapling in her vacation. As it was very hot she had to water it daily. Slowly her interest in the plant wore off after a few days. She forgot to water it for many days. I showed her the drooping leaves and said, "See how thirsty your plant is, it is wilting. It cannot speak out to you, but how can a plant survive without its food?" My daughter instantly felt sorry. She is extra careful about plants now.

12. Giving Real-life Examples

In summer vacations, I found my thirteen-year-old daughter to be short tempered and tense. Deeper probing revealed that she was anxious over her performance in swimming lessons. Despite a week of coaching, she could only float. I told her my own experiences in swimming. It had taken me three days to let go of the edge of the pool and stand straight. It took me two seasons just to learn dog paddling. She burst out laughing on hearing this. Her spirits lifted and she became a confident swimmer soon.

Sometimes, recounting experiences from your life helps the children in facing problems. Recount your own experience with a problem and how you tackled it. The outcome of the problem should be positive. The children realise that nobody is perfect and you have to work hard to achieve a goal.

My husband recounted to my son as to how he was careless with his tools and how all of them rusted. His father refused to buy anything for him till he took better care of his things. My son polishes his tools diligently.

13. Delayed Reward of Greater Attractiveness

Sometimes, a delayed reward of greater attractiveness can help encourage appropriate behaviour, and discourage inappropriate behaviour. A child has a bad throat, cold and cough. He insists on having ice-cream as the other children around him are enjoying it. He can be promised a triple 'sundae' instead of a single scoop if he follows the doctor's diet and recovers from his illness. The child happily suppresses his immediate demand.

"If you secure 85 per cent marks or above in the annual assessment by working hard throughout the year, I will buy you a home computer." This statement by the parents is sure to motivate the student to work hard regularly. When a child does achieve his target, be sure to give him his reward. Try not to break promises. Children are trusting souls but start mistrusting people if they are not true to their words.

'Promise of Future' rewards can be used effectively with adolescents. You can tell your teenaged children that if they resist smoking and drinking till the age of twenty-one, they may be given a vehicle of their own. By that time, they are mature enough not to be addicted to these vices.

14. Tackle the Problem

Sometimes, a child faces a problem at school, home or play, which results in inappropriate behaviour. If the problem is solved, it puts an end to such behaviour. Choose one problem at a time. Try to think calmly about it. You can tackle it in three steps.

Karan is unable to finish his home assignments on weekends.

- Brainstorming – Think of a number of possible solutions to the problem. If the child is old enough, he can participate by giving his own solutions. Consider the advantages and disadvantages of each method.

- Choose a solution – Choose a solution which is acceptable to the child. The child has to cooperate.

1. Karan will show his home task to his mother on Friday.

2. They will assess the approximate time required to complete the work.

3. On Friday, two hours will be devoted to the assignment.

4. He will do the oral revision work on Saturday and finish rest of the written work.

5. He will not go for outing on Sunday till all the work is complete.

15. Write a Contract

Written word carries authority. It is always easier to remember things if all the points are written down. It will be quite helpful to the child if everything is put in black and white.

Choose a habit which causes you maximum anxiety or leads to maximum conflict with the child:

- Write down in clear terms what you want the child to do.
- Who will check his habit?
- Time and date from which the contract will be effective.
- Go over the terms with the child, and make him understand those fully.
- Reward for appropriate behaviour.
- Negative consequences, if the child does not show the desired improvement.
- Changes can be made by discussion and mutual consent.

For example, Tarun, aged ten years, always returned home from school with his tiffin intact. He used to be irritable because he remained hungry. He had many excuses for not eating his lunch: "I did not like the lunch packet", "I was too busy playing", "I did not get time to eat it", and so on.

In such a case, the contract framed will comprise the following terms:

- Tarun has to finish his tiffin in school everyday.
- His mother will give him a list of options which can be prepared conveniently in the morning, e.g. sandwiches, French toast, vegetable poha, parantha.
- Tarun will tell his mother what he wants to have for lunch, a day earlier.

- Mother will check his tiffin everyday for leftovers.

- If Tarun finishes his tiffin daily, he can decide the menu for Sunday morning breakfast.

- If he does not, he will not be taken out for ice-creams on Saturday, along with other family members.

Similar contracts can be put down for other problems too. For a child who is reluctant to help with the household chores:

- Ankita will dust the drawing room on Sundays.

- She will dust the furniture, show pieces, doors and windows.

- Mother will check to see if the dusting is done properly.

- If Ankita does her chores well, she will be taken to her favourite pizza joint in the evening.

- If she does not do so, she will miss her outing.

16. Good Conduct Chart

This is an easy and enjoyable way to help the child. This method is sure to yield good results, especially for pre-schoolers and school-going children of all age groups. Prepare a short list of three to five good target behaviour patterns. (Keep the problem behaviour in mind, e.g. carelessness). The objectives of the expected behaviour patterns should be clear and well defined. For example, 'Behaves well' or 'Helps in the household chores' are general terms and very difficult to evaluate. Some expected outcomes can be: "Puts his toys away after playing", "Cleans his school shoes", "Dusts the furniture", etc.

Prepare a chart on a drawing sheet as shown below:

S. No.	Target Behaviour	Mon	Tue	Wed	Thu	Fri	Sat	Sun
1.	Puts his toys back.							
2.	Finishes his meals.							
3.	Does his homework.							
4.	Cleans his shoes.							
5.	Hangs his towel.							

The left-hand column carries the desired objectives of the target behaviour pattern. Next to it are seven little columns for every day of the week. In this way, an 8×5 grid box is made. This chart can be hung in the child's room, door, or wall.

If the child accomplishes a task, a gold star is made on the chart. After a week, the total number of gold stars are counted. Sit with the child and decide about the fair rewards for good behaviour. The maximum number of gold stars that can be obtained in a week are, of course, 35. Establish clear-cut incentives with the child.

No. of Gold Stars   **Incentive obtained**

25-30   -   Buying a favourite book, cassette, fancy pencil box, etc.

30-35   -   Going to watch a children's movie, beach, amusement park, bowling alley or family picnic.

Scores below 25 do not count. Still, you may want to give a consolation prize for a score from 20-25 to encourage the child. It can be an ice-cream scoop or a slab of chocolate.

Start marking on the chart from Monday onwards. At the end of the week, the number of gold stars obtained by the child can be counted and the child can be treated on Sunday evening. As the child's behaviour improves, a fresh list of goods can be chosen, e.g. "Speaking in polite tones", "Playing with younger brother or sister".

The child will try to better his score all the time but do not expect miracles. It takes time. Later, the target behaviour becomes part of normal behaviour. Later, wean the child away from this.

Giving Yourself a Lift

Ways to Relax to Cope with Child Rearing

1. Relaxation Exercises – Need for Relaxation

Are you experiencing irritability, anger, anxiety, and depression? Your emotions reveal that you are stressed out. Stress can produce indecisiveness, lack of concentration, lack of control and negative thinking. Isn't it time you take a break?

What is your concept of relaxation? Going to the hills in the summer break or lying on the beach with a book and a cool, refreshing drink? Is it something that we plan to do later? Is it something to be done when we finish with all our work? Do you think our work is ever going to be finished? Most of the time we keep postponing our seizure – outing.

Relaxation is something which we require on a regular basis. Try not to overreact to certain situations. You have a choice as to how to respond to a certain situation. Relaxation helps in taking the focus away from the source of stress and increases the possibility of experiencing a positive emotion.

Try to spend at least ten minutes each day in relaxation exercises like deep breathing.

Deep Breathing Exercises

- Sit comfortably in your chair.
- Close your eyes.
- Keep your arms by the side of your body.
- Remove all distractions from your mind.
- You are slowly feeling relaxed and calm.
- Rest your right hand on your stomach.
- Take a deep breath and feel your stomach rise.
- Now breathe out and feel your stomach go in.
- Repeat this exercise to a count of five.
- Slowly open your eyes – you feel relaxed and alert.

2. Meditation

Whenever we overstrain the human machine, i.e. the body and disregard nature's warning, the mind or body can suffer a breakdown. Meditation teaches us to be at peace with ourselves. It teaches us to be calm and experience absolute relaxation. 5-10 minutes of meditation can train the mind to be still and quiet. This stillness can be incorporated into our daily life by making us less reactive and irritable. Rather than seeing everything as an emergency, everything should be treated coolly.

Meditation is not easy. The moment you try to clear your mind of thoughts, it will be flooded with more unpleasant thoughts. Make a conscious attempt to blank out all thoughts. Beginners may be able to manage it just for a few seconds. Patience and consistency will help you increase this time. A few minutes devoted to meditation will pay you rich dividends.

This is how you can go about it:

- Choose some quiet environment.
- Close your eyes and sit cross-legged.
- Relax your muscles.
- Breathe through your nose.
- You can focus your attention on one point, which can be a picture, an idol, sculpture or even your breathing!
- Reciting the 'OM' mantra also activates the various centres of the central nervous system.
- You can recite a mantra, like the Gayatri mantra, by which one secures highest knowledge through God.

3. Yoga

Yoga is based on ancient Indian wisdom and culture and is more than 5,000 years old. Millions of people all over the world are using the system and discipline of yoga for self-evolution and self-realisation. Yoga is a totally integrated system which studies man in his wholeness, body, mind and spirit.

Yoga therapy is based on four important concepts of Ahar (diet); Achar (relationship or code of conduct); Vichar (thought process) and Vihar (a balanced programme to handle the body-mind complex, rest and recreation). This holistic approach restores balance and brings about harmony between the body, mind and soul.

Yoga gives one a feeling of peace, harmony and tranquility. It strengthens the muscles, creating flexibility and ease of motion. It is a tremendous stress reducer. A person feels more alive and focussed.

Some points in favour of yoga include:

- It is easy to do.
- It takes up only a few minutes every day.
- It is non-competitive and non-stressful.
- People of any age can do it.
- You can work and progress at your own pace and comfort level.
- It can be done alone or along with a friend or even with the family.
- Classes are held at local parks, temples, community centres.
- Yogic method of harmonious and deep breathing brings about a sedative effect on the nerves and helps achieve mental equilibrium.
- It is suitable for all kinds of people, e.g. harassed housewives, troubled parents, busy executives, and growing children.
- It is best to practise yoga exercises early in the morning or evening.

4. Take a Break

One day I rang up my sister, a senior consultant in a multinational company and a mother of two, an energetic three-year-old and a one-year-old kid. "How is the big boss?" I asked. "Boss, my foot! You are actually speaking to a slave. I feel I work round-the-clock. With the hectic office work and kids, I am totally fagged out by the end of the day. I become irritable and snappy by the night. My kind of entertainment is sleeping peacefully at a reasonable hour." She needed time-out desperately.

Everybody needs and deserves a break. Sometimes, a problem is not so urgent that it requires immediate solution. It is best to take a break from a child or even a spouse. Take a brisk walk without dwelling on the problem. With a clear head, then work on the problem.

My sister hit upon a plan to take a well-deserved break. On Saturdays, the children would be the father's responsibility for two hours. She would drive to the nearby beauty parlour. She would take a prolonged body massage, facial, pedicure, and manicure. These two hours rejuvenated and revitalised her.

Taking a break from parenting becomes a must sometimes. It is a never-ending job. You require time out not only to cope with physical fatigue but also mental fatigue. Choose an activity which you enjoy the most. It can be catching up on the latest bestseller, going bowling, going to watch a play or a film. Choose a person whom you can trust the children with. It may be the *dadi, nani, masi,* maid or a babysitter. Enjoy your time-out and face each new day with a fresh mind and right attitude.

5. Boost Your Self-image

Recently my doctor sister got a distress call from a friend, a brand new mother of lively nine-month-old twins. "The twins are driving me up the wall; if one is quiet, the other is cranky; if one is sleeping, the other one throws a tantrum. Sometimes, I just feel like tossing them out of the window. Is it natural for me to feel this way? I wonder why I went in for parenthood. It is a non-stop, full-time job. I feel overworked and unappreciated. Do you think I don't have the proper maternal instinct?" She gushed on unhappily. She was on the verge of tears.

"No, your reactions are absolutely normal. A new mother experiences physical as well as mental stress. Your problems seem more because you are handling two children of the same age together. In fact, you deserve a lot of credit for raising two healthy, lively infants together," said my sister.

Whenever you are feeling down and out, just consider the following points and boost your self-esteem:

- I love my children.
- I am a good parent.
- I am doing my best.
- I work hard.
- I am friendly.
- I can make my own decisions.
- I can control my anger.
- Everyone makes mistakes.
- We should learn from our mistakes.
- My children love me.

These positive affirmations will keep you going when you are down and need comfort. They work wonders when said by your spouse, sister, mother, or friend. The greatest morale booster, I feel, is one's own mother. Ring up your mother. Her five minutes of pep talk can work wonders for your ego. In fact, after the chat you will start feeling like a super mom or dad.

6. Share Your Problem

Sometimes discussing your problem with others helps. In India, we have a strong family support system consisting of *dada, dadi, nana, nani, tau, tai, chacha, chachi, masa, masi, mama,* cousins, etc. These people may be living with you or near you. They can offer you invaluable advice on how to deal with certain problems. There may be no single magical solution to your problem but talking with them will certainly lessen your doubts, fears and concerns. Grannies and granddads after all are the ones, who have scores of years of experience behind them.

When you are discussing your problem with a relative or a friend, he should be a patient and sympathetic listener, be available to you readily, should not criticise you, and should not ask for any favours in return. Talking to her or him can make you feel lighter and lower your stress level.

Nowadays, with distances growing wider in cities, neighbours can prove to be better friends than relatives. Ten minutes of exchange of problems over the fence may make you feel calmer. Active participation in parent-teacher organisation can also help solve many of your disciplining problems. Parents of children in a similar age group have similar problems. Discussions in small groups can be very useful. The child's class teacher is an important person who can throw light on the child's behaviour in school. Talk to her if your child faces any problem in the school. She may be able to pinpoint the reason behind the difficulty. The school guidance counsellor can also be consulted when needed.

Nowadays, in India, we have many hotlines that one can turn to in times of crisis, like Vimhans, Sanjivani, Sahara, etc. They help the child cope up with academic failures, loss of self-esteem, social maladjustment and negative views of life. These associations are flooded with calls, especially before and after the board exams. They have been known to do a lot of good work, especially for the teenagers.

7. Letting Anger Take a Back Seat

What is anger? Anger is basically a conflict of needs. We become angry if we think that someone or something is interfering with our wants or needs. Some individuals have a low annoyance threshold, while others can tolerate more provocation. Some others tend to bottle up their anger and explode like a volcano at a later date, venting their fury on one and all.

One of our biggest challenges is to express our anger in a constructive way. For this to happen, we must first learn to communicate with others in a sensitive and effective way.

Let us try to see why we get angry:
- Due to excessive physical and mental fatigue.
- Expecting others to read our minds and knowing what we need.
- Unrealistic expectations from everyone.
- Inability to say 'no' to others.
- Excessive delay in a happening.
- Inappropriate behaviour exhibited continuously.

How can we deal with anger constructively?
- Try to make peace with your anger by feeding yourself healthy thoughts. Try to make concessions for others' behaviour, e.g. your son could be very angry because his team lost the match in school or the baby might be acting cranky because it did not get its proper sleep.
- Try to avoid thinking in terms of right and wrong, e.g. it is bad to scream; it is right to be patient. Sometimes, a little bit of letting off steam may even prove to be healthy.

- Focus on one problem at a time. Juggling with too many conflicts at the same time can leave you unhappy, tired and solutionless. Tackle the most important problem first, e.g. child's truancy.

- Choose an appropriate time: If you are angry or tired, do not try to work out a problem, e.g. sending the child to a boarding school as a form of punishment for misbehaviour.

- If possible, communicate and express your feelings with whom you have a problem. When your child speaks to you in an insolent way and challenges your authority, tell him that you feel very hurt and would not like a repetition of such behaviour.

- Express your needs in a clear and simple way, e.g. all the household chores are not your responsibility alone. Make your stand clear. Tell them that you also feel tired and need leisure time.

- Be specific in what you want the other person to do or not to do. For example, for a boy of ten years, you can set the following tasks:

  ◆ Water the plants on alternate days.

  ◆ Keep his desk neat and clean.

  ◆ Clean the dining table after having food.

  ◆ Not to stay outdoors after 7.30 p.m.

- Use reflective listening: Many times when we are listening to others, our minds are elsewhere. Repetition of what the other person is saying helps the other person in realising that you are sympathetic to his cause.

- Do not attack or blame the other person. If a child breaks an expensive vase while playing with a ball in the dining room, it is better to say that this wouldn't have happened if he had followed the rule of playing in the garden.

Look for solutions: Try to look for all possible solutions to the problems instead of aggravating them further by shouting or hitting.

Reciprocating anger with anger will only fuel more anger. In contrast, a calm, sympathetic response makes it difficult for the other person to maintain his rage.

Excessive anger in the house can create an atmosphere of tension, fear, and mistrust. It can make the person feel lonely and isolated. At the same time, anger can play havoc with physical health. Chronic anger can lead to severe headache, hypertension, and ulcers etc.

Control over anger is a must for effective parenting.

How to Shape Your KIDS Better

—Hari Datt Sharma

It is in the parents' hands to mould their children into perfection

Children are like wet cement, whatever falls on them makes an impression.

—Haim Ginott

Parents often have a tendency to blame children for their failings—little realising that their own role in their personality development is of much greater significance than their offsprings'. Parents need to look within to see how they can be model parents and provide a healthy environment for proper mental, emotional and physical growth of their children. Focussing on this basic issue, this book holds a mirror to parents, and shows how they can excel in the art of parenting. However, over-protection or restrictiveness can spoil a child; permissiveness or indulgence can make him anti-social, rejection can work on his personality—why he takes to lying, stealing or mud-eating. This book is a total guide to the subject covering topics from effects of disturbed parenthood, role of right communication, common childhood behaviourial disorders like stuttering, bed-wetting, nail biting to behaviour improvement techniques, skill development, fostering creativity and helping in setting and achieving of goal—and finally a complete section on looking after handicapped children.

Demy Size • Pages: 124
Price: Rs. 68/- • Postage: Rs. 15/-

The Joy of Parenting

—Sangeeta Gupta

A comprenensive parenting guide covering infancy to adolescence

In the days of yore before the advent of television, the Internet and other extraneous influences, parenting was a simple task, especially in a joint family milieu. Today, bringing up children is a more arduous, complex and delicate task. The common-sense guidelines in this book will ensure you maintain just the right balance between firm and flexible parenting, as per the attitude, aptitude and ability of your child.

Besides negative influences from the electronic media, children are especially vulnerable to peer pressure. How you handle your children during their formative years can make all the difference between having courteous, well-adjusted children who respect elders, peers and friends or being saddled with ill-mannered kids who are a law unto themselves.

The book covers all the important aspects of childrearing to help you become a role-model parent.

Demy Size • Pages: 144
Price: Rs. 80/- • Postage: Rs. 15/-

Parent's Gift to a Child

—S. Devaraj

The book is aimed at instilling into every child a challenging attitude to dream of even the unlikely with a certainty feeling and to face even the impossible with possibility thinking.

This book has a magical power to make every child believe that the easiest to fetch is success and the closest to reach is happiness. It can exercise upon every child an irresistible appeal for stainless thinking, truthful talking, tireless sweating, rightful dealing, selfless loving and joyful living. It can also inject into a child, a longing to love God wholeheartedly.

Pages: 88
Price: Rs. 50/- • Postage: Rs. 15/-

Mummy, I'm Hungry!

—Juhi Aggarwal

A practical guide to child nutrition

*M*ummy, I'm Hungry! As a young mother, how often you hear these words... For mealtimes can be the most challenging time for any mother, and feeding an infant or toddler calls for more than just preparing any ordinary meal. It requires imagination to prepare meals that are both tasty and nutritious. Since the health and growth of your child depends largely on nutritious meals, what, how and when to feed you child is of special significance.

The infant's diet also calls for a slow transition from mother's milk to liquid diet, from liquids to semi-solids, from semi-solids to a soft diet, finally culminating in normal family meals. The book outlines this transition with meticulous care. The recipes chosen are wholesome, covering a variety of food in order to develop their taste buds. They are easy to prepare and based on homemade ingredients— unlike market food that contains harmful preservatives and additives. Alternatives are given at the end of each recipe. Not only does this book provide guidelines for lifelong healthy food habits developed in the child's formative years, it ensures delicious meals for the child with a growing appetite.

Demy Size • Pages: 136
Price: Rs. 80/- • Postage: Rs. 15/-

Practical Parenting Tips

—Vicki Lansky

***Over 1,500 Helpful Hints
for the First Five Years***

Here are just a few of the ideas in this book that parents have actually used to make life with young children easier:

Child proofing:
Keep valuable and small article away from baby's reach. Drape a towel over the top of the bathroom door to keep children from shutting it tightly and locking themselves in.

Tantrums:
Listen. Acknowledge the source of frustration. Whisper in your child's ear. The screaming may stop or turn into a giggle. Disappear into another room. You'll feel better and the tantrum will lose steam.

Hair Care:
Sit your child in a high chair to prevent "wandering." Spread a newspaper underneath.

Remove gum from hair with peanut butter. Work it into the hair and then comb out both gum and peanut butter.

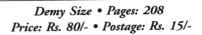

***Demy Size • Pages: 208
Price: Rs. 80/- • Postage: Rs. 15/-***

Baby Record & Photo Album

A baby is not a vase to be filled, but a fire to be lit.

—*Rabelais*

Your baby is your priceless possession. You have noted down a few particulars of his birth and taken a number of snaps and put them aside. Your baby's particulars could get mixed up in the grind of day-to-day work.

Have you ever wished to treasure the precious moments of your baby's birth, his growth and development?

Ever felt the need to have an illustrated and articulated album to record your baby's particulars right from his birth?

Well, **Pustak Mahal** brings for you the **Baby Record Album**, where you can jot down the particulars of your neonatal's arrival, his health record, the gifts he received on his birth, particulars of his naming ceremony, the family tree and *mundan* ceremony, with space to affix his lock of hair.

The album also provides space to record details about your baby's health, a vaccination table, and important milestones about his growth. It also gives space to affix photographs.

The **Baby Record Album** is a must for every family to record their baby's development. You will reminisce with nostalgia when you sit back and turn the pages of the album after your child grows up and strives to find a place of his own in the society.

Big Size • Price: Rs. 125/- • Postage: Rs. 20/-
Also available in Hindi

Raising a Daughter
in 21st Century India

—*Rupa Chatterjee*

The mother of two daughters, the author has used both, her own experience and suggestions from peers, to give valuable insights on bringing up a daughter in 21st century India. She has not only attempted to highlight the problems of bringing up a daughter today, but also tried to show how these can be tackled and how the best of our traditional values can be combined with current requirements to bring up a well-adjusted daughter.

The book contains time-tested tips, sane suggestions and reliable recommendations, with insights from paediatricians, psychiatrists, teachers and other experts, and will serve as an effective guide for all mothers, particularly first-time mothers.

Peppered with numerous first-person accounts, *Raising a Daughter in 21st Century India* can serve as a handy guide in moments of trying tension, while dealing with your teenage daughter.

Demy Size • Pages: 136
Price: Rs. 80/- • Postage: Rs. 15/-

The Art of Successful Parenting

—Shalini Mitra

How to behave so your children will too

Being a successful parent is hard work. Raising well-behaved children requires courage and patience. Some parents believe that love is enough to have nice, lovable children. Love is essential but it is not a guarantee for good behaviour.

Well-behaved children are the result of good parenting. Parents and children are partners in discipline. Parents need training just as professionals need training. Training gives you confidence. You learn that what you are doing is right.

As you read the ideas in this book, you might say, "Sounds great", "That will work for me", "Yes, it happens with me, too". Reading about a new technique is not the same as practising a new technique. Practising a new idea means changing your behaviour.

This book contains ideas, strategies and techniques that you need to use more. The book does not focus on what children do wrong. It teaches parents what they can do differently. To correct your children's behaviour, you first have to correct your behaviour. You will also find that many of your present ideas are appropriate and need no change. In short, this book will give you a fair idea of how to behave, so your children will too!

Demy Size • Pages: 140
Price: Rs. 68/- • Postage: Rs. 15/-